Guyana Ve:

A Church of England Mission

John Twisleton

Commendations for
Guyana Venture

Guyana Venture provides an invaluable record of the dedication of those who answered their calling to serve their Church in South America, amongst whom was numbered John Twisleton himself.

We are indebted to John for this highly readable account of the stories and sacrifices of his fellow missionaries, set against the background of a country moving out of colonialism and into nationhood.

Philip Harris
Chairman of Guyana Diocesan Association 1994 - 2000

I am a Guyanese living in the UK for twice as long as I lived in Guyana.

This book fills in many gaps in my knowledge about Guyana in general and the Diocese of Guyana in particular. It covers some of the most difficult political years, of Guyana's emergence into Independence and an uncertain future.

Fortunately, as documented herein, the Diocese of Guyana was very richly blessed with extraordinarily committed spiritual leaders.

Errol Ganpatsingh
Formerly member of Guyana Diocesan Association Council

Fr Twisleton has produced a highly informative and valuable work which will greatly interest current and former members of Guyana Diocesan Association, especially those who generously and sacrificially supported the Association's finances in those dark and worrying days in the 1980's when almost on a weekly basis barrels of food, clothing and toiletries were being sent to Guyana from the UK to alleviate the plight of the people. Solar lamps, outboard motors and ecclesiastical supplies were also sent on a regular basis.

All that magnificent financial aid was underpinned by the prayers, interest and goodwill of so many people and churches, for which God be thanked.

Fr David Maudlin SSC
Treasurer of Guyana Diocesan Association 1982 - 1998
Commissary to the Bishop of Guyana 1996 - 2015

4

Foreword

This is an account both historical and personal of noble endeavour over many years.

Anglican Guyana has been fortunate in two lengthy episcopates, Bishop Austin's 50 years in the 19th century, and the towering figure of Bishop Alan Knight in the 20th century, who leaves an example of ministry still felt today.

Colonialism was often marked by cruelty and greed but this is an antidote, an account of personal sacrifice before and after Guyana's independence.

The personal accounts here of both John and Anne Twisleton are valuable historical records. Some of the priests from the Company of Mission Priests who are profiled here I have known personally, and their commitment to mission was undimmed in 'retirement'.

The Alan Knight Training Centre may have closed, but its legacy continues to this day in the Amerindian churches and in their priests, now often senior in years, who show the same sacrificial spirit as they minister in the interior. The consecration of one of their number as a bishop marks a fitting testimony to the work recorded here and the promise of a new venture.

+ Peter Wheatley
Formerly member of Guyana Diocesan Association Council

Contents

Title page

Commendations 1

Foreword 5

Introduction 8

1   El Dorado 12

2   Behold a great priest 18

3   Guiana becomes Guyana 24

4   John Dorman - English Saint 30

5   Derek Goodrich - Anchor Man 36

    Photographs with captions 42

6   The Alan Knight Training Centre 54

7   Colourful Trio - Fathers Cole, Heal and Holden 62

8   Missionary pot pourri 68

9   The Twisleton venture 74

10   Venturesome faith 80

Conclusion 86

Notes 90

About the author 92

Books by the author 93

Introduction

Follow me and I will make you fish for people Matthew 4:19 (NRSV)

The beauty and challenge of Guyana, formerly British Guiana, has drawn a succession of missionaries from the Church of England to South America. This book complements Blanche Duke's 'A History of the Anglican Church in Guyana' in telling something of that history from the English end (1). An Englishman who has 'eaten labba and drunk creek water' and been made a Canon of St George's Cathedral, I have a lifelong bond both with Guyana and the Anglocatholic faith of my fellow missionaries. 'Guyana Venture' is framed by my service to the Diocese of Guyana and my spiritual friendship with Canon John Dorman and Dean-emeritus Derek Goodrich. The book charts my personal adventure, including my marriage to Anne at Yupukari, whilst addressing two centuries of missionary enterprise. Closure of Guyana Diocesan Association (GDA) in 2022 was a milestone in this mission partnership of which my book is a celebration.

GDA and I go back over 40 years to the friendship I built with John Dorman. It was he who planted in me the idea of investing a period of my life in Guyana to build on the work of other missionaries training priests supported by GDA and its partner the then-styled United Society for the Propagation of the Gospel (USPG). By 1987 12 indigenous candidates had been formed as priests so the sacraments were available regularly across most of Guyana's interior. The invitation, which I took up with Fr Allan Buik and my wife-to-be Anne, at the Alan Knight Training Centre at Yupukari, was to lead training for a second group of six men. These were fishermen before they were priests and fishermen in another sense after their priesting in 1990. 'Follow me, and I will make you fish for people' Jesus said (Matthew 4:19 NRSV). Over the years I have spent involved with GDA I have reflected on the different scale of evangelistic fishing in England and

8

Guyana. The priests I trained have both rivers teaming with fish and communities readily caught up into worship when there is a priest 'to fish for people'. On every visit to Guyana I am made aware of the contrast in the size of congregations there and those in the Church of England. The Diocese of Guyana is not short of 'fish', to continue the analogy, though she could always do with more 'fishermen'. There remains a great shortage of priests although recent years have seen new vocations. It was refreshing, as priest used to small congregations, to sweat away at giving Holy Communion to hundreds of folk week by week. I recall one Sunday Mass in Guyana when I emptied the Tabernacle and had to re-consecrate twice to provide for the multitude that flocked to the rails. On another occasion I recall 1000 young people aged 15-30 turning out for the annual Diocesan Sports Competition, something most heartening at a season when the Church of England was losing 1000 young people every week.

'Guyana Venture' researches the Church of England mission to British Guiana, later Guyana, starting from 1781 up to the closure of GDA in 2022. It is no exhaustive study but a personal one with broad brush strokes linked to the author's limited perception. The book is a fruit of the investment of my life in the Diocese of Guyana from 1986, training priests, visiting to serve mission and ministry there at the invitation of successive bishops and working with GDA Council to facilitate exchange of gifts and personnel supportive of the Diocese. That support of Anglican work has been respectful of the variety of religions serving Guyana's diverse peoples, notably of Indigenous, African and Indian heritage. One privilege of living in Guyana is the mutual respect evident there between faiths and increasingly between diverse racial groups. Despite the misuse of power during the colonial era many Guyanese keep affection for the UK and the Commonwealth. Though now part of the Church in the Province of the West Indies (CPWI) the Diocese of Guyana similarly retains an affection for the Church of England, which will survive the demise of GDA, especially gratitude for its contribution to raising up priests to serve Guyana's vast interior. This work was crowned by the consecration by Bishop Charles Davidson of an indigenous assistant bishop, The Right Revd Alfred David, in 2021.

The book has ten chapters starting with the origins of British Guiana, the telling myth of 'El Dorado', the heroism of pioneer clergy and the long reign of Bishop William Austin. Chapter 2 entitled 'Behold a great priest', antiphon sung to welcome Bishops in Anglocatholic parishes, features Archbishop Alan Knight who built up the mission partnership known as GDA attracting key personnel from overseas to serve the Diocese. Chapter 3, covers the transition to independence as Guyana, growth of self sufficiency in the Diocese and the reign of Randolph George as first native Diocesan Bishop. Chapter 4 centres on the saintly John Dorman's mission within Guyana's interior affirming Amerindian culture, paving the way for indigenous priests and inspiring service by priests from overseas. In Chapter 5 consideration is given to the missionary contribution of Dean-emeritus Derek Goodrich whose gifts helped anchor the Diocese, GDA and many individuals on Christian basics. Chapter 6 focuses on the achievements of the Alan Knight Training Centre (AKTC) for Amerindian clergy set up by the Company of Mission Priests (CMP). Chapter 7 profiles Frs Cole, Heal and Holden and Chapter 8 some shorter term 20th century UK missionaries. In Chapters 9 and 10 my wife Anne Twisleton and I write about our time at AKTC and follow up visits to Guyana under the auspices of USPG and GDA. The book concludes with a reflection on the providential rise and fall of GDA.

In writing 'Guyana Venture' I have drawn extensively upon the writings of my late friend Derek Goodrich and his collection of GDA's El Dorado magazines. My aim is to complement Blanche Duke's great work on the Diocese of Guyana. Her book provides invaluable detail of church development whereas mine profiles the contributions of a handful of English missionaries known to me directly or indirectly through trusted sources. I apologise in advance for neglecting other significant missionaries due to my own ignorance of them, despite research, and also lack of available documentation. In celebrating the mission of GDA and its associates my book aims to encourage mission partnership of equals across the world geared to building up the body of Christ in faith, love and numbers.

The harvest is plentiful, but the labourers are few; therefore ask the Lord of the harvest to send out labourers into his harvest Matthew 9:37-38 (NRSV)

Canon Dr John F Twisleton
Feast of St Matthew, 21 September 2022

1   El Dorado

I wear a wedding ring made with Guyana gold. Throughout my time in the Rupununi I came across miners drawn to Guyana's interior by the lure of gold. The lost city of gold called El Dorado was associated with the parish I served which witnessed a flow of European treasure hunters from 1492 when Columbus came on the South American scene. Literally meaning 'Golden Man' El Dorado has also been associated with legendary kings of the Muisca people populating the northern Andes who were initiated by being covered in gold dust before leaping into Lake Guatavita. The gold lust impacts to this day the indigenous people of Guyana adversely caught up for centuries in the quest for gold and the conflicts associated with it. Mitchell Henry writes in 1990 of the honouring of a pioneer Church of England missionary who stood up for the Amerindians in the Rupununi:

'Thomas Youd Church, Kaicumbay was blessed by Bishop Randolph on November 29th 1989... The mission 2 hours drive from Yupukari has 60 members and is named after an English Missionary, the Revd. Thomas Youd, who made his presence felt among the amerindians of the Rupununi sometime during the early 19th century. That was a time when the Brazilians would capture the indians and take then as slaves. Thomas Youd fought for their protection, writing to the Governor of British Guiana, Sir Henry Light: 'what jealous eye some of the Brazilians look upon me with...fearing that all their capturing expeditions will have to come to an end, and that they will finally lose some of their fancied possessions... I would humbly request... that Your Excellency will favour me with a letter of protection, with a Portuguese translation, giving me authority to continue the work of instruction amongst the Macushi Tribe of Indians living at Pirara etc." Extract dated March 6th 1839. Thomas Youd Mission began without a Church building. Under the wise and capable leadership of Catechist Alexis Vincent a splendid thatched Church has been built up by villagers, encouraged by AKTC personnel who have conducted three confirmation training weekends. The bishop confirmed 19 adults the day he blessed the new Church and 8 couples have been married there already in the short time it has been standing. All praise to the faithful of Kaicumbay, and praise to the Lord they serve who has so blessed their labours. Postscript: Thomas Youd received a stipend from the Diocesan Office 100 years after his death. This happened when a cheque for Catechist Alexis Vincent was written to Thomas Youd instead. Man is not infallible!' (2)

One of the first Church of England missions to the interior of British Guiana was complicated by a dispute between Britain and Brazil both laying claim to lands associated with 'El Dorado'. The saintly Church of England missionary Thomas Youd saw his mission at Pirara (Yupukari) closed by the Brazilian government and died shortly afterwards. Blanche Duke's History records: 'Around 1832 twenty-year-old Thomas Youd arrived at the Bartica Mission station. Soon he was left on his own as the priest, Rev. Armstrong, he had come to help was "invalided home". Youd became "schoolmaster, sick nurse, doctor, captain, architect, boat-builder, mason and blacksmith". Though he travelled to Indian settlements up the rivers he adhered to saying morning and evening prayers and learning Akawaio, Carib, Macushi Languages and even Creole Dutch. He too had to face tragedies - his nephew who came to assist him died here, as did his first wife and his infant son. After the return of Rev. Armstrong to Bartica, Thomas Youd concentrated on the remote settlements travelling as far as Apoteri and into the Rupununi where his second wife died probably from poisoning. Youd himself weakened by malaria, it is assumed, died at sea in 1842 on his way to England. The Rupununi Missions languished after Youd's departure. The Guiana Diocesan Church Magazine of March 1895 relates a re-opening of his Mission and this eventually became the site of AKTC (1984-1990). More details of what she calls 'Nineteenth Century Stalwarts' are provided by Blanche Duke especially Revd William

13

Henry Brett (1819-1886) ordained priest 'for 40 years a Missionary of SPG... the Missions at Cabacaburi and Waramuri are a visible monument of his patient and self-denying toil. When he came to the Colony in 1840 there were none but pagan Indians in those rivers: now it would be difficult to find an Aboriginal Indian there who had not received Christian baptism' (3).

The year Thomas Youd died was the same year the Diocese of Guyana was formed through the consecration as bishop of William Piercy Austin (1807-1892) in Westminster Abbey on the Feast of St Bartholomew, August 24 1842. Austin's 50 year ministry as Bishop built upon the work of military chaplains and Bishop Coleridge of Barbados preceded by work among settlers on the Surinam River and founding of St Bridget's Church, Paramaribo in 1651:

'The foundations of the Anglican Church in Guyana, or as it was termed in those early days, the Church of England in Guiana, were laid in the period 1781 to 1814. Much of this early history of the church is connected solely with the names of naval and military Chaplains who... were appointed in Georgetown and New Amsterdam to minister to the English. Some of them did missionary work among the Negroes, but it was not until 1824 when Dr. Coleridge became Bishop that missionaries were sent out for that special purpose...prior to the creation of the See of Guiana (Guyana) in 1842, Bishop Coleridge of the Diocese of Barbados had the oversight of the Church's work in the colonies of Demerara, Essequibo and Berbice for 16 years... He paid pastoral visits 1826, 1833, 1836 and 1839, and travelled widely... dispensing the Word and Sacraments and perfecting the organisation of the Church with characteristic apostolic zeal' (4). Bishop Coleridge was assisted by the Church of England Societies for the Propagation of the Gospel in Foreign Parts (later USPG) and for Promoting Christian Knowledge (SPCK). These two societies supported me as a missionary serving in Guyana almost 150 years later with my wife Anne and most of the missionaries celebrated in this book. The former United Society has tellingly changed the third word of its title from Propagation to Partners in recent years expressing the humbler tone of outreach from the Church of England.

Described by a youthful Queen Victoria as 'the youngest and handsomest of my bishops' William Austin consecrated the first St George's Cathedral 1 December 1842 thereby conferring city status upon Georgetown. This happened five years after the emancipation of slaves among whom Austin had previously ministered as also among the amerindian peoples. At a time when premature death among missionaries, as with Thomas Youd, linked to the prevalence of malaria and yellow fever, was common, William Austin's 50 year episcopate was remarkable and reflects his notable physical and spiritual stamina. He led the Anglican Church through the heady post-emancipation period which saw a great influx of East Indian and Chinese immigrants many of whom found a place in the Diocese of Guiana. Austin made the church accessible by insisting candidates for the priesthood study Hindi and by using Chinese-speaking catechists. A great educationalist, Bishop Austin promoted the church's leadership in elementary education and helped the Diocese found Queen's College (1844) to serve secondary education and Bishop's College for training both priests and teachers.

'Bishop Austin then in his 85th year did not take an active part in the opening of the Cathedral in 1892. But it was also his jubilee (50 years as bishop), so Dean May who was one of the first ordinands trained at Bishop's College gave an address, in the presence of the Bishop, in which he recounted the following statistics pertinent to Bp. Austin's regime ' 'The clergy had increased from 24 to 40: six Archdeacons he had collated for Demerara and two for Berbice: 39 of the Clergy had been instituted to benefices: 98 had been ordained deacons and 81 priests: 41 places of worship and cemeteries had been consecrated and

15

37 Chapels licensed: and the number of the confirmed ran into many thousands'. On November 9,1892 Bp. Austin was laid to rest in the St. James-the-Less cemetery after many years of unstinted service in God's vineyard' (5). Austin House, the official residence of the Anglican bishops of Guyana is named after William Austin.

Archbishop Alan Knight looked to Bishop Austin as a model, writing: 'Bishop Austin made no attempt at any time to mould the Church in Guyana after the Church of England pattern. As he believed, the Guyanese Church must be given its own image and identity. It must be sound in Catholic Faith and Order but developing its own traditions and constitution to suit its own peculiar needs and local requirements. Bishop Austin was a Tractarian, a close follower of that small but influential group of scholarly divines in the University of Oxford who looked back to the age of the Fathers, and to the undivided Church of the early centuries, to find there the pattern in accordance with which the Churches of the Anglican Communion of their own day were to be fashioned in the true Catholic and Apostolic tradition... The main objectives of his policy throughout his long episcopate was to develop an indigenous church, self-reliant, self supporting and self-governing, witnessing to the Gospel and serving the people of the country as a whole' (6).

The Church of England ceded oversight of British Guiana when the Church of the Province of the West Indies became self-governing in 1883 and Bishop Austin was made Archbishop. From then on the Church of England became a mission partner though British Guiana's colonial government supported its Anglican Church until disestablishment in 1921. With William Austin's death the payment of the Bishop's salary from England ceased in a partial disendowment challenging to his successors led by Bishop William Proctor Swaby who consecrated the completed Cathedral, in 1894. 'The wooden church reaches a height of 43.5 metres (143 ft)... St. George's was designed by

Sir Arthur Blomfield and... has been designated a national monument... the first plans for the new cathedral were for a building in stone with a central tower and two western towers; but these were rejected because of the weight and the expense. Blomfield's subsequent plans for a wooden cathedral were accepted, a design that kept many of the salient features of his first plan, such as the central tower and the Latin cross formation of nave and transepts. It was in the Gothic style of architecture, complete with flying buttresses, but it also had a tropical flavour, ensuring light and air. However, it was to be in timber and the committee emphasised that "woods of the country and no others were to be used", although in fact pitchpine was imported from North America for the ceiling... St. George's was built mainly of Greenheart' (7).

With Blomfield's gothic edifice dedicated to England's patron St George the Church of England made its mark on British Guiana and the name of its capital, Georgetown. As a national monument pointing heavenwards it represents a high point of the Christian evangelisation of South America which rode awkwardly on the back of the seeking of El Dorado's gold, exploitation of human beings through slavery on the sugar plantations and bonded labour in the rice industry. Worth more than gold is the growth of churches born from the Church of England, many of which now exceed their mother's in size and vitality. More than that, the export of clergy and laity into the Guyana diaspora has brought blessings back to the UK, Canada and the United States, including for almost a century the mission partnership we call GDA.

17

2   Behold a great priest

'Behold a great priest' sang Catechist Justus Christian and we repeated the antiphon. Whenever the Bishop came to St Mary, Yupukari we rehearsed for days before the full antiphon used in catholic tradition to welcome our Father-in-God at the church door. The Bishop kisses the crucifix, sprinkles the people with holy water and is himself incensed. By the time I became parish priest of the Rupununi in 1987 this ritual was a fixture across the Diocese. It went back to the days of one who was a great priest not just as Bishop but as a physically towering figure and one whose flamboyant yet spiritual ministry was famous on either side of the Atlantic. Guyana Diocesan Association entered its own through the 42 year ministry of Bishop Alan Knight. This ascendancy grew out of GDA's modest creation during the 15 year rule of Knight's predecessor Bishop Oswald Hutton Parry (1921-1936). The latter succeeded an unrelated namesake, Bishop Edward Archibald Parry (1900-1921) following the reign of Bishop William Proctor Swaby (1893-1900) who succeeded Bishop Austin.

Derek Goodrich quotes Robert Moore on Alan Knight: 'A robust Anglo-Catholic, he made the Church under his direction one of the great centres of traditional Catholic ritual and devotion in the Anglican Communion. A convinced Caribbeanist, he liked to say that the Anglican Province of the West Indies was a lesson to the West Indian States on how to create unity in diversity. There were times when his behaviour was almost Papal, and yet he saw himself as a dyed-in-wool democrat. He was never an easy man to categorise... but there were two areas in which he admitted no contradiction: his faith in God and his love of Guyana' (8). Those words are a summary of the man responsible in more than one sense for my own call to the Diocese of Guyana. This was linked to the Diocese being infected by his 'robust Anglocatholicism' with a momentum that was to reach after his passing into Guyana's interior through his memorial, the Alan Knight Training

Centre I came to serve in 1987. As an Anglocatholic, that call to train priests for Guyana for me linked to the Anglican Church there being then 'one of the great centres of traditional Catholic ritual and devotion in the Anglican Communion'.

It should be noted that Catholicism is not equated to Roman Catholicism, important as that Creed is, nor is it to do with elaborate forms of worship i.e. "smells and bells" - Catholic worship can be grand or simple according to taste and occasion. To hold to the Catholic Faith is to hold to the mainstream of Christian belief as held in most centuries and over most of the world. Such Faith has a yearning after the "whole" and a disdain for what is partial, sectarian, parochial or one sided. Anglocatholics are concerned to witness to that broad stream of Christian believing that flows down through the Christian centuries of which the Anglican Church claims to be a part. On another analogy, the branch theory, the two Provinces of the Church of England and the Province of the Church in the West Indies stem from an Anglican branch of the 'one, holy, catholic and apostolic church' alongside the major Roman Catholic and Orthodox branches.

Alan Knight was brought into such faith through his involvement as a young man in the flourishing parish of St Jude-on-the-Hill, Hampstead Garden Suburb. He was a server there, was confirmed in 1916 and at school wrote a book of devotion for the newly confirmed used at St Jude's. After serving as a student teacher he studied History and Law at Cambridge where he was active in the Boat Club, hence the trophy oar later displayed at Austin House. From 1924 he prepared for the priesthood at Bishop's College, Cheshunt and was ordained deacon 1925 in St Paul's Cathedral. Derek Goodrich writes: 'He celebrated his first Mass on May 31 1926 in the Church of SS Peter & Paul, Enfield... this was a great event in his life, and he would celebrate over 19,000 Masses in his Ministry, the daily Mass being at the heart of his spiritual life... Fr Knight remained at Enfield for three years and then had a call

19

to work in West Africa where he was to live for nine years...serving as Headmaster of St Nicholas' Grammar School at Cape Coast in the Gold Coast of West Africa, now known as Ghana... [where his fundraising from home] resulted in the Archbishop of Canterbury pronouncing him 'the most successful beggar in the Church of England', and deciding that a priest with his talents was needed in British Guiana as Bishop' (9).

Within months of his becoming Bishop in 1937 Alan Knight encouraged the then Guiana Diocesan Association (GDA) to produce 'El Dorado' magazine twice a year communicating current affairs of significance in the Diocese to UK parishes. GDA's primary object was stated as to 'advance the Christian religion in particular by supporting the work of the Church in the Diocese of Guyana in the Province of the West Indies' working in cooperation with the USPG and serving fellowship between citizens of Guyana and the UK. Alan Knight served this mission partnership as a writer, teacher and traveller making El Dorado a 'must read' in many UK parishes. In a 1955 talk on vocation Alan Knight stresses the value of the celibacy which he himself clearly followed. This availability to the Church facilitated his going almost everywhere in Guyana's extensive interior, to other Caribbean dioceses after he was made Archbishop (1951), making regular visits to the UK fostering GDA and on occasion to Ghana. Bishop Alan Knight became within a few years of moving there an extraordinary advocate for Guyana, Christianity within that land and Church of England funding and personnel for the Diocese of Guyana through GDA. His ministry emerged at the apex of the Anglocatholic revival and drew a succession of Tractarian or Anglocatholic priests across the Atlantic who in turn drew me to serve under his successor, native Guyanese Bishop Randolph George. I think of Allan Buik, Richard Cole, Brian Doolan, John Dorman, John Fowler, Derek Goodrich, Jack Holden, Ken Livesey, Donald Percy, Peter Peterken and Arthur Whitehead among close acquaintances of whom Frs Dorman and Goodrich need special attention in my 'Guyana Venture' alongside my colleague Fr Allan Buik. All of us have been privileged to engage in the spiritual and ecclesial buoyancy of the Diocese linked decades back to Knight's teaching, pastoral and administrative acumen. In his Foreword to Derek Goodrich's 'Words and Works of Alan John Knight' (1999) Robert Moore recalls Knight's parody of St Paul's saying 'Brevity, cogency and clarity, these three are the principal virtues in writing. But the greatest of these is clarity' (10).

Bishop Knight gave clear teaching allied to concern for church unity and the pastoral care of individuals. In the Diocese of Guyana the Provincial standard on the indissolubility of marriage - the Province of the West Indies dissented from the 1948 Lambeth Conference's allowance of remarriage after divorce - was upheld to counter the illegitimacy rate. In Guyana the discretion of the Bishop to admit to Holy Communion those remarried after divorce was NOT exercised in Alan's reign. 'In 1971 in reaction to a proposed re-examination of the law concerning abortion, he was outspoken on the subject. "The practice of abortion is, and will always be, a grievous sin for which those concerned will have to answer before the judgment seat of God. Legislation cannot make the act any less sinful." There was a difference between a sin, which is an offence against God and a crime, which is an offence against the law of the land. The practice of abortion was morally wrong and was nothing less than pre-meditated killing. He did admit there were certain agonising situations as when the life of mother and child were both in danger and it appeared impossible to save both, or in a case of rape or where the child was unwanted and might be deprived of care and love. However his legalistic training came through when he said that "hard cases make bad law". On the subject of Obeah, he was equally blunt: "No Christian could practise it without denying the Faith and no Christian could be harmed or influenced by any Obeah practised against him, because God is stronger than all and at the sign of triumph Satan's host doth flee'. Evil men may do what they will but we are safe in the arms of Jesus". He attacked the view that Obeah was a part of Guyana's national culture and questioned from his African experience whether Obeah in Guyana belonged to African tradition... The Archbishop lamented the increase in the number of suicides, which were a measure of the degree of tension and frustration existing in the community. Suicide was a product of escapism and although many were mentally ill, others were in need of a friend or confidant to whom they could unburden their minds. The worried person could be assured of God's own promise "My strength is sufficient for you: in quietness and confidence shall be your strength". He stressed the role of the Clergy in giving support to those under stress: "Go out into the darkness and put your hand into the hand of God; and that shall be to you better than light, and safer than a known way."....

'In 1977 the Archbishop spoke on the greatest problem facing the Anglican Communion, the Ordination of Women. The Parishes had been asked to study the issue, but little concern was manifested. He found it shocking that some Provinces of the Church, notably in North America, had rushed into the Ordination of women in a way that 'must be regarded as irregular, even if not invalid, to the distress of our brother Christians of the Roman and Orthodox Communions and to the embarrassment of many Anglicans whose consciences have been affronted'. He insisted that it was not a question of whether Congregations would like to have women Priests, still less whether a majority would desire this, nor whether it would be expedient or for the benefit of contemporary society; but only whether it was the will of God and in conformity with the pattern of the Church as ordered by Christ. He pointed out that Our Lord chose no women as Apostles and strongly attacked the idea of a progressive revelation as if Christ's knowledge on earth was limited. This he felt had led to 'unwarrantable extravagances as for example in the recent Marian dogmas formulated by the Roman Communion, in the teachings of the so-called Modernists and in the pronouncements of some of the Protestant theologians. These grave departures from the Faith once delivered to the Saints have contributed to the opening of the way to the Ordination of women'. He found most of the official statements on either side "inadequate and unconvincing".... the Archbishop being assailed by a Jamaican Deaconess on the matter of the equality of the sexes, and therefore the Ordination of women, being a matter of justice... closed the conversation with "Of course men and women are equal, but they are not identical". It is likely that Alan Knight would have accepted the Ordination of women if it was the act of the whole of Catholic Christendom, but he could not accept unilateral action by the Anglican Communion, let alone by individual Provinces and Dioceses... [He wrote]: 'The purpose of the Church can never change, but the methods by which this purpose is to be accomplished must always be changing. The Faith can never change, but it has to be differently interpreted to succeeding generations if it is to be understood and made acceptable. The moral law is insurmountable but sociological changes frequently demand a review of the application of Christian principles to new situations' (11).

3   Guiana becomes Guyana

This well written précis history of Guyana at the back of GDA's El Dorado of September 1968 possibly written by Alan Knight himself captures this extraordinary land drawing a succession of missionaries from the Church of England over two centuries: 'The country lies on the north-east coast of the South American continent, between Venezuela on the west, Surinam on the east, with the Atlantic Ocean facing it on the north. It is as large as the combined areas of England, Scotland and Wales, or about twenty-four times the size of Puerto Rico. It has pleasant climatic conditions for the greater part of the year. It is particularly so on the coastal area where it is sub-tropical. Columbus sailed along the Guyana coast in 1498, and later wrote about the great rivers of Guyana flowing down from an earthly paradise. Some Portuguese traders, by 1580, had built a fort up the Essequibo River. They traded with the Indians. Sir Walter Raleigh voyaged to the country in 1595. The task of shaping Guyana's history was shared among the Dutch, French and British. Both the Dutch and British made the greatest contribution, each holding the country for well over one hundred years, compared with the short two-year period of the French. As a consequence, the impact of the former had been the stronger. Between 1841 and 1931 some 433,643 immigrants arrived in Guyana on the basis of an indentureship system. Two points - one of economic significance, the other of sociological importance - have been introduced into Guyana as a result of this huge slice of imported manpower into Guyana. The East Indians and West Indians went into agriculture (coconuts, rice, coffee and limes in addition to sugar). The Portuguese gravitated towards the retail business established by hucksters who were mostly free-coloured women of African stock, and helped to expand it. Today, this pattern is much more flexible. Chinese and East Indians are also within the category. A number of people of African descent went into mining - for gold, diamonds and bauxite, and the collection of forest products such as timber and balata. Here too, the present day workforce has ceased to be the haven of a special section of the population. A more cosmopolitan complexion is being taken on. The Government of Guyana now proclaims to the world the latest developments in mineral exploration in rapid succession molybdenum, copper, gold, nickel and zinc prospects have appeared. Wherever shouts of "Gold! Gold!" were raised, history provides evidence of men flocking thither. Guyana has not been the exceptional case. Already, three internationally famed companies are undertaking all exploration activities along the Guyana coast. Guyana is not an illiterate country. The literacy rate is about 80 to 90 per cent, one of the highest in the world. Education begins from the kindergarten level and ends at the university. The Technical Institute, with branches scattered about the country, caters to the development of craft skills. A college of agriculture is disseminating modern techniques in farming and animal husbandry. Faculties within the country's University provide training for future geologists, technologists and administrators. This, then, has been the story of Guyana. Guyana the New Nation on the brink of Promising Frontiers, is confidently moving forward into the world with the determination to do well' (12).

A brief sketch of the transition from British Guiana to the Republic of Guyana, not shy of the politics, is provided on Britannica.com: 'From 1953 to 1966 the political history of the colony was stormy. The first elected government, formed by the People's Progressive Party (PPP) and led by Cheddi Jagan, seemed so pro-communist that the British suspended the constitution in October 1953 and dispatched troops. The constitution was not restored until 1957. The PPP split along ethnic lines, Jagan leading a predominately Indo-Guyanese party and Forbes Burnham leading a party of African descendants, the People's National Congress (PNC). The elections of 1957 and 1961 returned the PPP with working majorities. From 1961 to 1964 severe rioting, involving bloodshed between rival Afro-Guyanese and Indo-Guyanese groups, and a long general strike led to the return of British troops. To answer the PNC allegation that the existing electoral system unduly favoured the Indo-Guyanese community, the British government introduced for the elections of December 1964 a new system of proportional representation. Thereafter the PNC and a smaller, more conservative party formed a coalition government, led by Burnham, which took the colony into independence under its new name, Guyana, on May 26, 1966. The PNC gained full power in the general election of 1968, which was characterized by questionable rolls of overseas voters and widespread claims of electoral impropriety. On February 23, 1970, Guyana was proclaimed a cooperative republic within the Commonwealth' (13)

The evolution of the Cooperative Republic of Guyana out of the colony of British Guiana was therefore something of a roller coaster with Britain not deferring from intervention in the colonial democracy at the behest of the United States. Archbishop Alan Knight was unexceptional as a cleric of his day in teaching Communism as a form of godless materialism to be countered. In 1953 Knight wrote critically of the left-leaning PPP government suspended by Britain. Though a bishop of CPWI, Knight was trained in the Church of England and in those days Church and State were very close and shared power especially in the colonies. The Anglican Church was to pay a price for its association with Britain, especially the interventions in 1953 and from 1961 in the run up to independence. As a teaching bishop Alan Knight did not refrain from instructing the Anglican faithful about moral principles, the need for voters to form their consciences and clergy to refrain from involvement in party politics. Though he never commended a particular party his justification of the suspension of the Constitution was seen as inflammatory by some. He wrote of the PPP government being a 'sorry story of one disgraceful episode after another, the failure of the Ministers to do anything constructive, the fomentation of unjustifiable strikes, the stimulated growth of class consciousness and racial hatred and the deliberate use of threats and organised intimidation by the

26

Party to overcome all opposition and even to silence the voice of fair criticism.' Though Knight justified Britain suspending the Constitution and taking emergency measures in 1953 he emphasised 'the need to plan a stable economy and to accelerate development to provide employment and to raise the lamentably poor standard of living.' There was a need to restore democracy and to bring healing and national unity in place of racial strife. Archbishop Knight wrote that the crisis had 'aroused people to a sense of their responsibilities and has brought an awakening to many Christian consciences. God always does bring good out of evil. I believe the Church will emerge stronger from this period of trial and testing' (14).

The loosening of the Diocese from the Church of England had led to a financial and human resources crisis and it was Archbishop Knight especially who brought creative ownership of this crisis. The failure to value freedom by taking responsibility for things somewhat anticipates the later crises that flowed creatively out of national independence. 'In his Charge to Synod 1971, Archbishop Knight disclosed the dire consequences that came in the wake of Disestablishment. He said, "This year, 1971, is the 50th year since the Disestablishment of the Church in the Diocese of Guyana ... The record of the first 15 years of Disestablishment is nothing of which to be proud. The members of the Church of the period apparently failed to appreciate the value of the independence which they had gained and were either insensible to their new responsibility or unwilling to pay the price of freedom. The Administration of those years followed a policy of defeatism and endeavoured to balance the budget by a systematic reduction in the financial commitment. Mission stations were closed, the work of the Church in most areas was contracted, and when priests who had been on the Establishment retired or resigned their places were not filled. Thus, while the Diocese had 42 Parish Priests on the Staff in 1921, by 1936 the number had been reduced to 17. Even this parsimonious policy failed to resolve the problem of maintaining the work and witness of the Church, by then deprived of financial support from Public Funds, and by 1936 there was debt of some $17,000 on the current account... By the mercy of God, the Church in Guyana then came to itself. The debt was paid off and the decision was taken to restore the clergy to its full strength as quickly as possible." Blanche Duke continues: 'The Diocese from between 1936 and 1966 worked hard to balance the budget year by year. With few exceptions parishes paid their quotas of Assessment and the Diocesan Fund remained in credit. Restoring the number of Parish Priests to a "workable figure" took longer than was anticipated though the staffing situation showed steady improvement. It took until 1970, nearly half a century, to equal the 1921 total of 42. But the work of the Church had been widely extended and the population had almost doubled itself so that the staff once again numbering 42 was inadequate still. A worthy feature is that there have been more indigenous clergy than in the early years after Disestablishment... The present staff [in 2000] is predominantly Guyanese which seems to indicate that the Church in Guyana is "truly established" since it has provided almost 90% of its Sacred Ministry from its own local membership. The Bishop, the Dean, the Vicar General, the Rural Deans and four of the six Canons are all indigenous' (15).

Independence saw Guyana welcoming its first indigenous bishop when Archbishop Knight headed up the consecration of Philip Elder as Suffragan Bishop of Stabroek 20 February 1966. This action greatly extended episcopal ministry into Guyana's vast interior preparing the way for a further extension of indigenous ministry through the calling out of vocations to the priesthood from Amerindians not least through Knight's memorial, AKTC. When Bishop Elder moved from Guyana in 1976 Archbishop Knight ordained Guyanese Cathedral Dean Randolph George as his Suffragan. This paved the way for leadership of the Diocese of Guyana to be local parallel to the national leadership of Guyana born out of British Guiana. In 1980 Randolph George was

28

enthroned as Bishop of Guyana. On that occasion he said: "Today's ceremony of Enthronement marks the beginning of a new phase in the life of the Anglican Church in this Country. We remember with gratitude today the labours of my predecessors in office especially William Piercy Austin and Alan John Knight of revered memory who between them guided the Anglican Church in Guyana with distinction for ninety-two out of one hundred and thirty-seven years' existence as a separate diocese. Because of what has been handed down to us, I can make the words of the Psalmist my own. 'The lot is fallen unto me in a fair ground: yea I have a goodly heritage'." He at the same time added, "I am under no illusions. We live in difficult and trying times in which all the qualities of constructive leadership required of a bishop of the Church in Guyana are put to a severe test." His text however came from Ephesians 6:10 "Find your strength in the Lord, in his mighty power." In many ways, including devout Anglocatholicism forged in Church of England curacies, Randolph George built on the legacy of Alan Knight establishing AKTC, ordaining the first Amerindian priests, raising up honorary (non stipendiary) priests and speaking truth to power at a difficult season in national life. George's commitment to social justice led him to work with his brother Roman Catholic Bishop Singh for 'free and fair elections' which occurred in 1992 and he was asked to head a national Commission on Race Relations (1993). Bishop George with his Church of England service was an enthusiastic supporter of GDA regularly visiting the UK especially CMP parishes so that I trace my own calling to be a missionary in Guyana to his invitation following that of Canon John Dorman CMP.

4   John Dorman - English Saint

'It will afford a good idea of the proportion which imaginary danger from animals in Guiana bears to the real evils inflicted by these if we try to realise the possible thoughts of a nervous man when bathing in one of the rivers of that country. The nervous bather remembers that from the moment when he throws off his clothes, every part of his body not covered by water is exposed to the attack of mosquitoes, sandflies, and many other sharply stinging insects; but, on the other hand, that every part of his body covered by water may at any moment be bitten by perai, may receive a violent shock from an electric eel, or may be horribly lacerated by the poisoned spine of a sting-ray, or a limb may be snapped off by a passing cayman or alligator, or his whole body may be crushed, and thus prepared for swallowing by a huge water serpent; or, even if none of these pains come upon him, he may remember that the egg of a certain worm... may be deposited unnoticed on his flesh, there to develop and become exceedingly painful. Now all these dangers are real enough, and any one of them may make itself felt at any moment. But on the other hand, of all the men who trust themselves in these waters day after day, and many times a day, for years together, not ten per cent, have ever felt even any of the smaller evils which have been described, except perhaps the bites of mosquitoes or sandflies; and not one in a thousand has suffered any serious or permanent harm. While therefore the nervous man feels all the pain of anticipation of evils, neither he nor the less timid man as a rule feel the actual evil (16).

Few less timid men have existed than John Dorman who bathed in the rivers of Guyana for forty years and braving such risks drew many others there including myself. My sub-title 'English Saint' is allied to conversations about John Dorman (1916-1998), who died 18 July 1998 and whose ashes are buried in Kamarang, being submitted for inclusion in the Calendar of the Church in the Province of the West Indies. Though Fr John was awarded an MBE by the Queen his distinction is in another league, that of holiness 'the most powerful influence in the world' (Pascal). The passage about the risks of river bathing in Guyana from a 19th century explorer was handed me after John persuaded me to come and train Amerindian priests. I had recently joined the Company of Mission Priests (CMP) of which he was a founder member, someone we looked up to as a veteran missionary full of tales of the beauty and peril of Guyana's interior, though as with all saints some found his enthusiasm disconcerting. In social gatherings Canon Dorman was a striking figure with a direct gaze that seemed to go to the heart of each one of us in his company. His evangelical fervour linked to the prayerful anglocatholic faith typical of CMP. This Church of England mission body was founded 1940 after the outbreak of World War II after an appeal by Superiors of the Religious Communities at Cowley, Kelham and Mirfield (SSJE, SSM and CR) supported by a covering letter from the Archbishop of Canterbury, Cosmo Lang. 'There was a need, they said, to form a company of Mission Priests, who would undertake to remain free from the personal and financial obligations of marriage and family life so that they could work, if necessary, without a full stipend, and be available to go wherever they might be needed. In this way, the pastoral and provision made for the future growth of the "housing estates which threaten to become new centres of heathenism." These Mission Priests, the Appeal suggested, would not take vows, as members of the Religious Communities did, but would bind themselves to this form of Apostolic Life by a solemn Promise to be renewed annually; and could withdraw from the Company on giving the required notice. A number of priests responded, and the first members [including John Dorman] were admitted on the 2nd of May 1940. By 1944, the Company had 26 members... Since then, the Company has continued to serve both Church and people, primarily in the large housing estates and inner-city areas of England, but also, for many years, overseas, in Guyana and Madagascar' (17).

31

In the 21st century the word 'missionary' is an uncomfortable word in a world so much more aware of the variety of cultures and religions. We doubt the unique claims of religion. We question whether human well being is advanced by religion. We are particularly uncomfortable with the British colonial legacy and its associated commendation of Christianity. With John Dorman I am proud to be part of the rich legacy of service the Church of England has provided in its Guyana Venture. With all its failings that venture flows primarily from hearts seeking to build and not tear down, to serve and not to be served, counter to the negative overtones of the word 'missionary' in today's world. Fr John first went to the then British Guiana at the invitation of Archbishop Alan Knight in 1957 and served there almost continuously up to his death in 1998. Son of a priest, he had grown up in parishes in Sussex and Norfolk, gone to Keble College in Oxford and trained for the priesthood at Ely Theological College. Ordained to the priesthood 1940 in Carlisle Diocese he served with CMP at Maryport and then Threlkeld (1944-1957) in the Lake District. He was a great letter writer which helped him maintain many friendships including that of his Carlisle contemporary Sister Brenda of the Community of St Laurence at Belper who used to relay letters to me from our mutual friend. I have a heap of John's letters including those to her but not alas the letter that arrived on my desk at St Wilfrith, Moorends, Doncaster one day in autumn 1985. This asked me to prayerfully consider augmenting the CMP team in Guyana, currently himself and Fr Richard Cole, to serve the training of Amerindian priests. I could find no excuse, such was the spiritual force of Canon Dorman on that and so many other occasions, linked to his docile yet courageous flowing with the Holy Spirit. The need for Amerindian priests was evident. It is demonstrated by a record of one of John's tours of the Rupununi region before AKTC when he baptised more than 100 children, gave Holy Communion to over 1000 and heard nearly 100 Confessions. It was primarily through John's initiative with that of Archbishop Alan Knight and Bishop Randolph George that the Amerindian communities today have priests so that the Sacraments are now available to all Guyanese even those in the remotest parts of the rainforest.

In his book 'Old-Style Missionary - The Ministry of John Dorman, Priest in Guyana' Derek Goodrich tells a riveting tale helped by John's letters. It begins with a shipwreck on the Essequibo in which Fr John nearly loses his life on his way to take a Boxing Day Mass. He swims in the dark to safety on Calf Island where he says a 'Magnificat' in thanksgiving. Writing from his hammock in the vestry at Kurupung he speaks of the 'paint on the walls still scarred by the blood the vampire bats have sampled from my great toes'. As one once attacked by a vampire bat at Issano with that bloody sequel I can say I have been baptised in the same baptism of blood as my hero! Derek Goodrich describes how John was 'driven from the Mission one night by a pack of jaguars and on another occasion was arrested by the Venezuelan frontier guards on the pretext of teaching without authority on their soil, a trumped up charge fortunately soon withdrawn'. The missionary priest spends himself in much itinerant ministry: 'Towards evening he would reach a Mission for Evensong, Confessions, Confirmation class then sleep in a hammock with Mass in the early morning. The work was endlessly varied in pattern and human need "It is concerned with carrying the simple riches of divine love to the simple poor people who need Him," Fr John writes. "Could there be anything more at one with the work of the Gospel than a little boat full of silent and reverent people returning from their Communion, the priest barefoot in alb and stole sitting in the bow and carrying the pyx containing the Blessed Sacrament for some faithful sufferer to whom the Lord travels as on the sea of Galilee?" Fr Goodrich describes Canon Dorman's advocacy for Guyana's Amerindians who are faced with the challenge of integration with Guyanese society as a whole. They are challenged by mining and logging ventures that damage their livelihood. The pollution of the rivers by dredging for gold remains a very serious problem. Fr Dorman writes of how the Amerindians 'at every point...live in two worlds and more and more these two worlds are coming into collision with their own ancient way taking most of the knocks'. When I used to visit him in Kamarang he was always deeply concerned about the heavy drinking and the video shops opened for the mining fraternity and their effect on the indigenous people. The formerly tranquil community had more of the feel of the Wild West with young people being drawn into prostitution. Between 1975 and 1983 John was involved in a successful international campaign against a major hydroelectric project that would have flooded the Akawaio homelands including the sacred centre of the Alleluia Church. His refusal to condemn the Alleluia Church which holds many elements of Christian tradition (but with no bible or eucharist) contrasted with the negative attitude of other Christian Churches. Fr John succeeded in obtaining associate membership of the Guyana Council of Churches for Alleluia and encouraged his priests and people to hold joint membership. His largest church at Jawalla was built especially to accommodate the traditional Alleluia dance which would accompany or follow the Eucharist on great feast days. In his homily in St James, Islington at Canon Dorman's funeral Fr Allan Buik said: 'True to the best traditions of catholic Anglicanism, both in theory and in practice, he stressed the Creation and the Incarnation as well as the Atonement. His cherishing of God's creation and of the tribes among whom he lived earned him high respect from environmentalists and anthropologists as well as from Christians - Alleluia as well as Anglican....His devotion to his Amerindians could be paternalistic...(his) foibles were all facets of his love for the people to whom God had sent him, the people for whom he never stopped caring'. All through 'Old-Style Missionary' (18) there is witness to the infectious enthusiasm of its subject who drew out so many vocations to the praise and service of God including my own. The quiet humility of John Dorman is echoed in the style of Fr Goodrich which is unobtrusive, presenting material assiduously researched in a way that honours both his subject, their common Lord and their 'dear land of Guyana'.

As I visited John Dorman in July 1998 just before his death at the Middlesex Hospital I was able to remind him of how my encounter with him had transformed my life in two ways. Prompted by the Spirit, Fr John led me both to serve Guyana's Amerindians and to enter the state of marriage, sadly parting ways with CMP. Our son, James, then 8, known and loved by Canon Dorman, was at my side to greet him in those last hours. As I prayed journey blessings on this great priest, it was with a reminder that, as he went to God, he was leaving a life - James's - that would not have come into being without his intervention. Fr John had written to me some time before his death, reflecting back on his forty year journeyings in Guyana's interior: 'I have travelled enough and there is another journey some time that needs its own prayerful and penitent preparation, that one may come to it eagerly, for the meeting to which it may lead and the mercy it must need.' May the prayers of this saint continue for us now we trust he has arrived at that great destination 'where we shall see God as he is' (1 John 3:2).

5   Derek Goodrich - Anchor Man

When Fr Allan Buik and I first arrived in Guyana April 1986 we were placed in a Cottage beside the Deanery across a very busy road from the magnificent Cathedral. Thus began a friendship with Fr Derek Goodrich that was to last half my life. He used to say I was his only friend to attend his 70th, 80th and 90th birthday celebrations. More than that I was to hear his last confession and preach at his funeral. When I arrived in Guyana Derek was Dean of St George's Cathedral where he demonstrated fine stewardship of allegedly the largest wooden building in the world. I had come with Allan to exercise stewardship of a humbler edifice - the Church, Library and mud houses of Yupukari that made up the Alan Knight Training Centre for Amerindian priests in the Rupununi. As we came and went from the interior to Georgetown Derek was our anchor man - confessor, spiritual director and mentor - along with that other great expatriate priest Canon John Dorman. Later on his return to the College of St Barnabas, Lingfield from 2001 he played a key role in the mission partnership of Guyana Diocesan Association which predeceased him. Dean-emeritus Goodrich presented apologies to the special meeting assembled to agree closure three months before his death on 6 September 2021. Derek was born 94 years earlier in Thornton Heath, Surrey, only child of Hugh and May Goodrich who also became well known in Guyana. 'Hugh was the youngest of a large family. He lost a leg in the First World War, and, as a senior civil servant at the beginning of the Second World War, refused to serve in the War Office. He was transferred to the Probate Registry, and evacuated to Llandudno, where Derek spent most of his teenage years. Derek undertook National Service as an ambulance driver. After ordination, Derek served at St Andrew's, Willesden Green, for five years. Here, he met the then Archbishop of the West Indies, Alan Knight, who was based in Georgetown in what was then British Guiana. He was inspired to go there, in 1957 (19).

In his autobiography Derek tells the story of 43 years missionary service in the Diocese of Guyana where he served in parochial ministry progressing through the positions of Canon, Rural Dean, Archdeacon, Dean and Vicar-General to be awarded in 1992 Guyana's Golden Arrow of Achievement. Primarily Derek served as Cathedral Dean between 1984 and 1993 supervising the implementation of vital repairs to the allegedly largest wooden building in the world, and the necessary fund-raising. This was the Cathedral which witnessed first hand the emancipation of slavery in 1834. So many slaves flocked into the original Cathedral to thank God for their freedom that a cracking noise was heard from timbers strained by their influx. The legacy of colonial exploitation continues in the ongoing political turmoil of Guyana. Fr Goodrich writes: 'In the early 1960's British Guiana went through a very troubled period. The Jagan PPP Government caused much concern with their left wing policies and there was great reaction to their threatened take-over of Church schools. Their economic policies roused strong opposition in Georgetown and there was a long General Strike following the tragedy of 'Black Friday'. Even more serious was the growth of racial strife; there were many cases of violence and burnings and communities that had lived happily together for generations were now divided racially and many families were compelled to move. I remember taking the funeral of an Afro-Guyanese woman killed in the Sun Chapman explosion on the Demerara River and within a week burying a young East Indian boy, one of our servers, who was killed in the backlash that occurred in Wismar. This violence was largely politically inspired, the two main racial groups forming the backbone of the People's Progressive Party (PPP) and People's National Congress (PNC). Although most responsible people realised the madness of racial strife, prejudice remained and when the PNC took over the control of the Government, following the Proportional Representation manipulations of Duncan Sandys and the British Government, most East Indians felt themselves victimised and at a disadvantage. However, Political independence was to be attained in

1966' (20). Over my own years as parish priest, theological college principal and canon of the Diocese of Guyana I became aware of how the racial strife indicated between PNC and PPP split clergy and parishioners quite alarmingly and how Derek strikingly rose above the divide. I tried to do the same as my main work was with Amerindians, a group distinct racially from the major blocks, with issues of their own concerning exclusion which Derek was able to advise about. As his version of history indicates, caring for both Afro-Guyanese and East Indians, he anchored the Diocese upon pastoral care across races which he carefully and assiduously modelled. Most of the clergy looked up to him on that account, sometimes making it difficult for Bishop Randolph who was more politically involved especially in challenging the PNC to allow 'free and fair' elections. One of many amusing stories Derek told was of the day two boys passed his Rectory when he was working in the garden and one of them said 'Look, white man!'. 'That's not white man' his friend responded, 'That's Father'.

For me working as an anglocatholic in the Diocese of Guyana was home from home. In the Cathedral we had the Angelus, Stations of the Cross, Solemn Evensong and Benediction. Fr Derek helped me develop a less partisan approach with an eye to anchoring people in love for Jesus through getting them into scripture. Seeing Jesus lifted up in both word and sacrament was transformative for him. It filled any spiritual emptiness he felt with grace, setting his heart back into a forward looking aspiration also pulling forward those of us privileged to be in his circle. Derek lived and taught the good news at the heart of Christianity hidden in the action of the eucharist pleading Christ's sacrifice for our sins, receiving the bread of his body to give life to our souls and through us to a hungry world. The Diocese being in catholic tradition was also blessed at one time with nuns as Derek records: 'The Sisters of the Community of Jesus the Good Shepherd were making a great contribution to the life of the Diocese especially with St. Gabriel's School which gained an outstanding reputation. Their Superior was

38

Sister Emma, small in stature but great in personality and leadership. One day she asked me to act as Games Master for the boys. I realised this was not an invitation but a divine command! As a result, I cycled to Queens College ground each Monday at 1.30 p.m. under the tropical sun to lead the boys in cricket and football. I also acted as Chaplain to the Sisters for a few months' (21).

Blanche Duke writes: 'Fr. Derek Hugh Goodrich retired in 1993 after 36 years of mission in Guyana... he always retained the "...vision and drive tempered by humility and empathy which he demonstrated in his continuing role of parish priest - shepherd of his flock, spiritual guide, mentor, leader, teacher, motivator, counsellor and friend". He did outstanding work in the parishes of St. Philip, St. Margaret, St. Sidwell, St. Joseph, All Saints and the Cathedral as well as contributed to the "fostering of vocations to the priesthood". It seemed as if his involvement in the Diocesan Ordination Training Scheme, the Fellowship of Vocation, the Diocesan Commissions on Ministry and on Stewardship complemented his work in the area of the building and restoration of Churches. The renovated Cathedral stands as the acme of his achievements. This monumental task gained him national acclaim and recognition' (22). When you read Derek's full autobiography (23) you become aware of how his priesthood has served thousands to good whereas we who soldier on in the Church of England teach but hundreds directly in our post-Christian culture. 'Just before I retired I did some Maths and reckoned that I baptised over three thousand, presented three thousand eight hundred for Confirmation, married some nine hundred and fifty couples, conducted nine hundred funerals, celebrated Mass on fifteen thousand occasions, and, horror of horrors gave over ten thousand sermons and addresses. How much suffering I have caused!' Fr Derek so records a faithful teaching ministry that reaches as widely as any priest could achieve in a lifetime. He records many amusing incidents including this from a confirmation class: 'I was put in my place one day when in response to the question 'What are the three Orders of the Sacred Ministry?' I received the reply 'Stand up, let us pray, be quiet'! Out of the mouths of...!' Praised for the perfect timing he achieved at a great open-air Solemn Evensong Derek reflects: 'I have always been a stickler for time, even in an unpunctual society. That I suspect was why the Confession in the West Indies Prayer Book was never transferred to the start of the Mass; otherwise some people would never arrive in time to make their confession!' His Church Times obituary notes: 'Derek believed that the Bishop of Guyana should be Guyanese, but was delighted to be invited to become Dean.. after which service he remained in Guyana for another seven years, as Priest-in-Charge of the open-air chapel of St Aloysius. By then, he had taken on two dogs, who moved into his seat whenever he moved out of it during services. He then enjoyed more than 20 years in retirement at the College of St Barnabas, Lingfield, and helped to lead worship for nearly the whole of that period. In 2015, he reflected: "I have been blessed with many great friends at the College. . . I have always regarded myself as a parish priest. For me that has been the best job in the world." (24)

'To the thirsty I will give water as a gift from the spring of the water of life. Those who conquer will inherit these things, and I will be their God and they will be my children' Revelation 21:6 NRSV. Preaching at Dean-emeritus Goodrich's funeral I said 'Our reading opens up the inheritance Derek thirsted for. Over his long life he built that thirst among thousands in the dear land of Guyana. He taught people about the God-shaped hole within them, the need to declutter it by repentance and to welcome the Holy Spirit. Living in divine mercy himself, this great priest infected you with the generosity that lives within and around us all. Even that abruptness, which cut you off in full flow to end the meeting or phone call, could be part of this when he spoke across negative or judgmental sentiments. Some things should never be voiced. Derek taught me to look on the best side of people and let their worst aspects be looked after by God who always treats us better than we deserve. Earlier this year Fr Derek was an enormous help to me in steering us through the closure of the Guyana Diocesan Association of which he like me had been a stalwart. Ever practical Derek saw clearer than most when a venture had had its day, had courage to say so and help imagine the best practical way forward within the possibilities of God... After his last confession, as Derek indicated gratitude to God for his long life and the gift of faith, among the last words he voiced were those of the Gloria in Excelsis - 'Glory to God in the highest and peace to his people on earth'. That is our prayer this morning, giving glory to God for a life well lived, praying peace upon Derek in paradise and, with resurrection faith, invoking the Holy Spirit upon ourselves and upon this troubled world (25)

James Twisleton, Fr John Twisleton & Jonathan Hawes
at Kaieteur Falls 2007

Fr Alfred David (2007) consecrated Guyana's
first Amerindian Bishop 2021

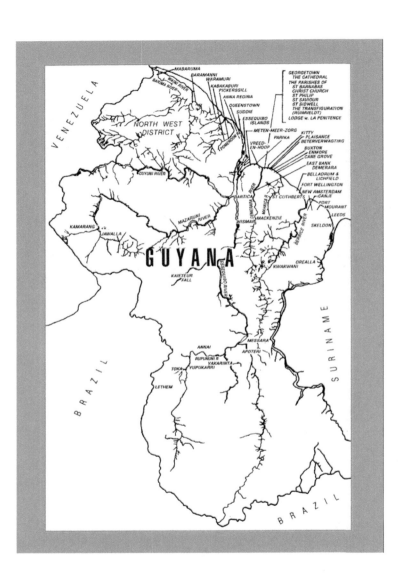

Victoria lilies in the Rupununi

Archbishop Alan Knight at the consecration of
Bishop Randolph George 1966

Fr John Dorman after arriving in British Guiana 1959

Canon John Dorman MBE in 1996

Dean Derek Goodrich in St George's Cathedral, Georgetown

Dean-Emeritus Derek Goodrich (80) in 2007

Ordination of deacons by Bishop Randolph George
at St Mary, Yupukari 1989

Frs Paul Richards, Jones Richards, Campbell Ewell,
Edmund Lewis, Mitchell Henry and Allan Alfred
after their priestly ordination in
St George's Cathedral 1990

Canon Jack Holden MBE visiting Guyana 1989

Fr Martin Heal (right) at St John the Baptist, Sevenoaks 1965

The Georgetown Sisters with Mother Superior 1975

Fr John Tearnan (centre) with Canon Dorman (left)
and friends at Kamarang

Fr John and Anne Twisleton married
at St Mary, Yupukari 1988

Canon Allan Buik (left) in 2004

Bishop Cornell Moss in Horsted Keynes (2011)

Canon Edwin Edwards, Jane Garner and Ulric Lyte around 2010

Bishop Charles Davidson at Horsted Keynes 2017

Sunset caught travelling home on the Rupununi River

6 The Alan Knight Training Centre

'Six am, cool and dark. The alarm clock is ringing and another day is about to begin. I climb out from under the mosquito net and hope the floor isn't covered with cockroaches, black beatles or any other delightful examples of tropical insect life. The clergy house now has a bathroom with running water and a flush toilet - so life is reasonably civilised. The church bell rings, that means 20 minutes until mattins. Few people have clocks or watches, so the bell really does call everyone to church. The students take it in turn to act as sacristan and bell-ringer, and whoever is on duty for the week has my spare watch to wear as a very practical badge of office.

In church the light is beginning to emerge from behind the Pakaraima mountains in the east. The angelus rings and the office begins. Lord open our lips': 'And our mouth shall proclaim your praise'. The divine office takes us up into its eternal rhythm, fitting the new day into psalm and scripture and praise. Mattins is followed by mass, when the students and their wives are joined by the villagers, so there are usually 30 or so of us each morning. Priest and servers go to the altar and the Holy Sacrifice is offered. At the offertory a hymn is sung, and the voices ring out around the quiet compound. Everyone gathers around the altar to feed on the bread of life, the bread which will strengthen and nourish and inspire the life of the day. There are plenty of boys keen to serve, so two assist each day - wearing knee-length green scapulars over their shirts and shorts.

After mass the school bell rings and the compound is full of cheerful children, just like a school playground anywhere. On Mondays the school day begins with flag raising and everyone singing the National Anthem 'Dear Land of Guyana' written by an Anglican priest. The school like all schools in the country is now government controlled, although it was built by the church. However, all our teachers are

Christians and worship in church on Sunday mornings, and the school day begins with prayers.

At 8.30 am the church bell rings again and the students gather in the church for half an hour of meditation and prayer. Despite the background hum of the nearby school, it is a time of peace and stillness, of listening to the still, small voice of God, and growing closer to him. Sometimes there is a spiritual address, but above all it is a time to be still and quiet. And it is soon over.

Then everyone moves across to the study and the day's classes begin. An hour and a half of Biblical studies. This term we are continuing to journey through the Old Testament, wrestling with the complexities of Israel's history with all those kings and battles. And the prophets thundering out the word of the Lord, the message of righteousness and judgement and repentance. And how their words ring true in today's world - social justice, materialism, the failure of men to live according to God's will and plan. Next term we shall move on to the New Testament and I suspect that everyone will be relieved and feel more at home.

At 10.30 am it's time for a break. A welcome cup of coffee for the lecturer and if there has been a shopping trip to Brazil the luxury of a biscuit. But not too many at once - a packet of plain biscuits costs over £1, so they have to last. Then back to the study. This term the second session has been devoted to a study of priesthood and ministry in the church. The students are beginning to realise the demands and complexity of being a priest and what a vital part the priest plays in building up God's people. The priest as evangelist, as teacher, as preacher, as reconciler, as a builder of the community. And a lot of discussion as to how an Amerindian priest should be a priest. How he is to exercise his priesthood within the framework of the life of his people with their life-style and traditions. The traditional English pattern of the vicar in his parish obviously cannot be transplanted and it is essential that it shouldn't be tried.

At noon the angelus rings, so we all stand and pray it. together, and then continue our discussions. By 12.30 everyone is more than ready for lunch. There is also the radio to be operated by pedalling like a bicycle. Sometimes Canon Dorman from Kamarang is operating and we can greet each other and pass messages from his ordinands to their families. Eventually the diocesan office hopes to have a set, so we can be told what is happening in town and how much money the parish still owes. be consulted. Also the Bishop can be consulted. But it is lunch time, followed by a siesta - not always very enjoyable as it is now very hot and the clergy house has a zinc roof which is too low, so it quickly becomes an oven. However a hammock on the breezy back verandah is very comfortable indeed.

Each week the students write an essay, and in the afternoons they come for tutorials. The essay is discussed and questions answered, problems can be aired and occasionally at least, solved. Each hour goes by very quickly, with a welcome break at 4 pm for the inevitable cup of tea. Through the kind generosity of friends in England it is sometimes Earl Grey or Darjeeling, otherwise it is Red Rose, the Guyanese version of Brooke Bond, or Brazilian Mate an acquired taste but interesting - and unusual.

Evensong is sung each day at 5.30 pm and into it is woven the work, study and frustration and joy which each day brings in its train. The Anthem of Our Lady reminds us that Mary has a special love and care for us and cherishes us with a mother's love. A time for intercession and to be brought close to all those so far away who are loved and missed.

And then the principal's private hour - woe betide any student who interrupts it. The bliss of a shower, followed by half an hour or so to relax in the cool evening, watching the sun set over the Kanuka mountains and to wrestle with the crossword in 'The Guardian Weekly'. Suddenly, darkness falls and it is time for supper. Rice and fish, or meat (if a cow has been killed at the parish ranch or the students have been out hunting), sometimes the joy of fresh mangoes or other delicious fruit.

Then time to read and to listen to the radio. The BBC 'World News' and 'News About Britain' comes through at 9 pm and on Mondays, there is 'Twenty Questions'; on Fridays 'Thirty-Minute Theatre; on Sundays a service, once a month from St Martin's-in-the-fields. Canon Austin Williams seems almost an old friend now.

By then time for bed. Down comes the mosquito net, into the cool sheets and sleep follows very quickly. Another day is over and in a few short hours another will begin. So we praise God for the blessings of each day and place ourselves in his hands as we prepare to face the challenges of the next'.

So wrote Father Brian Doolan first Principal of the Alan Knight Training Centre in June 1983 to USPG supporters including myself and my parish in Doncaster (26). Brian and co-worker Fr Donald Percy were my colleagues in CMP working alongside John Dorman and Richard Cole in the Diocese of Guyana. All four men were to impact me, not least through conveying vividly, as in this news sheet, the privilege and thrill of training priests in Guyana's exotic and challenging interior. 'Staggers on the Savannah' was AKTC's nickname taken from that of St Stephen's House, Oxford where its first Principal, Fr Doolan had been a student and from where he shaped the Anglocatholic syllabus and pattern of training captured in his report. Brian and Donald had left their CMP parishes in the UK to train as USPG missionaries flying to

Guyana to serve as Principal and Rupununi parish priest respectively 1982-5 based in Yupukari near the Brazilian border. Archbishop Alan Knight's memorial drew in personnel and funding from the UK to serve Knight's passion to develop pastoral and evangelistic work in Guyana's interior under the auspices of Anglocatholic vision. That vision was imperative to his successor Bishop Randolph George whose Diocesan synod approved AKTC, a theological college for training Amerindians to become priests. The decision to train men other than at the Provincial seminary, Codrington College in Barbados, respected Amerindian culture in which until recent years family life was inseparable from farming and the countryside. At the same time the training and syllabus of AKTC had full determination to form priests of the universal Church not 'local priests' even if many candidates were chosen at village meetings. Canon Dorman's involvement in developing the Interior Catechists' Training Programme was pivotal in raising up such ordinands as well as personnel to train as in my own case. Like the ordinands I was swept along by John Dorman, out of my comfort zone, into AKTC with its aim to bring the fullness of the church - the eucharist - down rivers through forests and savannah to every Amerindian settlement.

Settlements in Guyana's interior have people speaking up to nine dialects which sometimes put English into second place. A major challenge for AKTC was bringing Amerindians of such varied dialect together for 3 years to learn in English. This presented problems of inculturation as radical as those faced by the Church of England staff. In Fr Doolan's description of AKTC I (1982-1985) there is no common meal, something we achieved in AKTC II (1987-1990) through my wife Anne's working with the ordinands' wives to negotiate food preferences eg for or against fish with scales or skin. Many Guyanese coastlanders find the monotonous Interior diet of cassava and fish difficult though inevitable on account of the cost of transporting canned or bagged food from the coast, Brazil or Venezuela. This partly explains why AKTC training was done using USPG missionaries since in the 1980s no Guyanese could be found able and willing to lead. It represented an unfortunate paternalism towards Amerindians but this was the political and social reality of Guyana forty years ago. The choice of Yupukari for AKTC was meant to be protective of Amerindians but ordinands and families ended up being exposed there to the damaging incursions of miners from Brazil trading industrial alcohol for local handicrafts. Advantageously they used guns to shoot game targeted for millennia with bow and arrow. Though hunting and farming was planned as a key component of AKTC, scarcity of game, time taken travelling long distances to farms, endemic malaria as well as chronic drunkenness among villagers led to the reconsideration of Yupukari as venue after AKTC I. The cost of rebuilding AKTC elsewhere was deemed prohibitive so Allan Buik and myself were tasked with helping people cope with these difficulties. Though AKTC II started like AKTC I with twelve ordinands, only six survived the course somewhat linked to the chronic shortage of food. Nevertheless AKTC enriched the Diocese of Guyana with eighteen Amerindian priests most of whom have provided faithful service sometimes against heavy odds. These odds include leading their communities in tackling miners polluting their drinking water and logging firms with disrespect for Amerindians and communication problems with the coastal Church. Before AKTC cohabitation was the default of Amerindians so another challenge facing new priests on return to their communities was addressing this culture. At Yupukari during AKTC II we worked with the local priest on encouraging marriage, warning cohabitees that unless they accepted the sacrament of marriage they would no longer be welcome to receive the sacrament of Holy Communion. On a lighter note in 1988 I was joined by Anne, my fiancée and we got married in Yupukari. This led to people saying 'Father do what Father say!'. My marriage came about because Anne, widowed with two children and like me as USPG missionary only in Buenos Aires, was advised by the Bishop of Argentina that the marriage planned for after AKTC II should be brought forward for the childrens' benefit. This happened through the generosity of our friend Allan Buik. Though I left CMP the three of us worked well together.

7   Colourful Trio - Fathers Cole, Heal and Holden

Fr. Richard Cole (1908-1997)

In 1956 Fr Richard Cole joined the Company of Mission Priests' Clergy House at St. Saviour's, Hull. The three priests there carried the ideal of collegiality to the extent that not one of them would make any decision without first consulting the others. Tradition has it that the undertakers of Hull found making funeral arrangements at St. Saviour's somewhat frustrating! In 1958 the Lambeth Conference passed a resolution approving the use of artificial means of birth control for married couples. Archbishop Alan Knight of Guyana made it clear that the resolution was not acceptable in his diocese. Fr. Richard shared the Archbishop's convictions and volunteered his services to him. He was to spend the larger part of his remaining active ministry in Guyana. He began in 1961 at Bartica where he and Fr. John Dorman established a CMP House to serve the parish and its interior Missions... fostering and encouraging many vocations to the priesthood... Fr. Richard then spent some time ministering on the island of Leguan in the Essequibo before returning to Bartica as parish priest when Fr. Dorman moved to Kamarang. In 1972 Fr. Richard returned to England... for four years. But the lure of the Caribbean was too much and in 1976 he returned to Guyana to take charge of St. Matthew's Providence and St. Ann's, Agricola on the East Bank Demerara. Despite his increasing years his vigour was undiminished and he was a familiar sight dashing along the East Bank road visiting and taking Holy Communion to the sick. He was greatly loved by his people and as always fostered and encouraged vocations to the priesthood. He took a particular interest in the Amerindians and when the proposal was mooted to establish a seminary in the interior he gave it his enthusiastic support... Fr. Richard became one of Guyana's characters. He was once attacked by a youth in Georgetown who made off with his glasses. This was an affront not to be endured and Fr. Richard gave chase, caught the youth, soundly cuffed him and got his glasses back! His exploit hit the headlines and he became almost a national hero! His interventions at Synod and Deanery Chapters were always significant and he was constantly presenting papers on a wide variety of theological subjects. He produced a diocesan form for Stations of the Cross which continues to be valued in many parishes. His own predilection was for a traditional style of liturgy and he found the Revised Services of CPWI not entirely to his taste. He retained a strong traditional spirituality - he would not break the fast from midnight before Holy Communion and refused to say Mass after mid day. This meant that his parishes rarely experienced evening Mass (although he never minded other priests doing it) and the altars in his churches remained firmly attached to the east wall. At St. Agnes, Grove, the churchwarden kept an eye on the road as the time for Mass approached and if Fr. Agard appeared, the altar came forward. If it was Fr. Richard it stayed where it was! Fr. Richard celebrated his Golden Jubilee of ordination as a priest in 1983 at St. Ann's, Agricola, and the next year decided that the time had come to retire. He returned to the United Kingdom... but when in 1987 he heard that Dean Goodrich and another priest would be on long leave at the same time promptly offered to return to Guyana for six months at his own expense to supply for them. He took charge of the large parish of All Saints, New Amsterdam and served it with almost his old verve and energy. In 1993 he moved to Ellesborough Manor in Buckinghamshire, a home for retired priests where he settled happily, dying peacefully there in his sleep after a stroke on 15th November, 1997, aged 89. He is buried in the churchyard at Ellesborough with its superb view across the Chilterns. We thank God for every remembrance of a devoted priest and commend him to the mercy of God whom he loved so well and served so faithfully.' *Fr. Brian Doolan* (27)

Fr Martin Heal (1913-2009)

"Let your light so shine before men that they may see your good works and glorify your Father who is in heaven." Mt 5:16 This quotation from Holy writ is the most appropriate when writing about Guy Martin Heal who embodied the ideals of Christianity. He moulded and touched many lives, enabling them to make their choice of profession and encouraging many others to answer their call to the sacred priesthood. Through them his light will continue to shine. This is his greatest legacy. Martin Heal's 6 feet 4 inches gave him a commanding presence, but it was his outstanding, vivacious and infectious personality which worked like a magnet upon those with whom he came into contact. Martin had ample training for his life's work as a priest. Early in his life he joined the Church Army as well as a religious order and finally found his true calling, the priesthood. He embraced the Curé d'Ars as his mentor and displayed tremendous love for the Blessed Virgin Mary. Martin Heal journeyed to Guyana (Guiana) in the late 1940s after much discussion with the Bishop of Guyana, Alan John Knight and officers of the Society for the Propagation of the Gospel. Once in Guyana, Martin was sent to All Saints' Church in New Amsterdam, Berbice, as assistant priest to his good friend, Father Robert Gray. His notable work and numerous achievements in Guyana evolved around three parishes, the afore-mentioned, as well as St Aidan's Church, Wismar, Demerara River and Christ the King, McKenzie, Demerara River. As a builder and fundraiser, he was par excellence and possessed a wonderful rapport with people in all walks of life. After his second stint at All Saints' Church, New Amsterdam, Berbice, this time as vicar, he felt compelled to return to his native England. He opined that his work in Guyana was completed. Once in England he became Vicar of St John's, Sevenoaks, Kent and later Vicar of St Mary's, Munster Square, London; all the while wrestling with his conscience and awaiting direction from the Holy Spirit. After many years of faithful dedication to the Anglican Church, Martin Heal became a Roman Catholic priest. He remained a mentor and confessor to many until it became physically impossible for him to do active service. He died a happy man a week prior to his ninety-sixth birthday. Well done thou good and faithful servant. Requiescat in Pace.'

(28)

Canon Jack Holden MBE (1912-1996)

'Jack Hatherley Holden came from an old-established Hampshire family... In the last year of the Second World War, he set sail for what was then British Guiana in South America, two degrees from the equator and it was there that he found the love and joy of his life. In nineteen years of devoted service, largely amongst the Amerindian peoples, deep in the hinterland, bordering on Brazil and Venezuela, he travelled constantly through the bush on foot, horseback or by river to visit the Missions in his enormous parish. As a true missionary, he not only celebrated the sacraments and taught the Faith in every Mission Station and School, his love for his people embraced their whole life, medical care, educational facilities, improved methods of building, farming, animal welfare, social structures-anything and everything which could improve the quality of living for the Amerindians and at the same time preserving all that was good in their native culture, became the daily pastorate to which this dear man gave himself without reserve. It is very right and fitting that Church and State both acknowledge the depth and quality of his dedication - the latter conferring on him an MBE and the former creating him a Canon of St George's Cathedral, Georgetown. His Canonry meant more and more to him with the passing of time. Two years ago he felt constrained to return his licence to the then Bishop of London. When I pointed out to him that he must be in Communion with a Bishop if he belongs to the Church, he took a deep breath and with a faraway look in his eyes said, in his inimitable voice: "As a Canon of Georgetown, I am in Communion with the Bishop of Guyana!" After two decades of devoted service to God in Guyana, Jack returned to England and was appointed Vicar of St Andrew's Stoke Newington where an amusing incident occurred to do with Jack's parrot. One day, to his dismay, it escaped from its cage and Jack put a notice in the window of the corner shop, offering a reward of £50 for its safe return. Some days later, a lad turned up at the Vicarage with a parrot, and Marjorie, his sister, in Jack's absence, handed over the £50. On Jack's return home, his joy at the sight of this parrot soon turned to dismay as he realised it was not his bird after all. His parrot was very voluble, whereas this poor bird never said a word! However, hopes were raised a few days later when one of those dear old ladies which only Cockney London can produce, called to our Jack over the churchyard railings - "Ere Vicar, I reckon I've seen that parrot of yours, having a lark in the park with a pigeon!" She was right; it was caught and talking all the way home, restored to its rightful owner who gladly handed over another £50. You can picture our dear old friend saying solemnly - never mind, these two birds can keep each other company"... Knowing Jack Holden through the past 50 years, I found him caring and generous towards people, gentle and patient with animals and plants, positively addicted to cameras, radios, recording-machines and mechanical gadgets of all kinds, possessed of a phenomenal memory of computer proportions, with which he could demolish a contrary argument with anyone who had not checked their facts in every detail! This outward approach to Life around him was rooted in a deep love of God and a commitment to fulfil the Divine Will to the end of his days. This inner dedication showed itself from time to time in a refusal to accede over the meaning of a word or text in Scripture or some difference in theological opinion and many is the time I had to remind him that he had the obstinacy of not just one but a wagon load of mules!! I leave you with the mental picture of a tiny incident in the film "Bread Upon the Waters," filmed in Guyana about forty years ago, to illustrate the need for priests for the Church's mission, and Jack played the leading role, simply doing his daily job as a mission priest, deep in the South American bush, which he had to

66

leave for a week to attend the annual synod in Georgetown, over 200 miles away. In this film the head man of an Amerindian village was dying and needed the priest. One of the young men promptly volunteered to make the hazardous journey to Georgetown, where social customs are rather different from those in the bush Half a century ago it was accepted that you went to church on Sunday in your best clothes and wearing shoes, In the film, the young man reaches the capital city on the Sunday morning, tired and exhausted, finds the church where Jack is just about to take service, goes to the front pew, conspicuously ill-dressed for the occasion and barefoot. Jack's sharp eyes noticed the lad and he stopped before ascending the altar steps, took off his own shoes, smiled at the congregation and celebrated the Eucharist - barefoot! To me, that gesture by dear Jack speaks volumes about the man whose tired body will be laid to rest today.'
G. Martin Heal 6th March 1996 (29)

8   Missionary Pot Pourri

The CMP Connection

'The Company of Mission Priests is keeping its Jubilee this year, 1990, so it seems appropriate to record the long connection of the Company with the Diocese of Guyana. John Dorman came out in 1956; he went to the parish of Bartica and Bartica Missions... Richard Cole came out to join him at Bartica in 1961... allowed to be with him for a while, although he already had a curate, because one of the chief points of CMP is working together in Houses. However, after a year the Archbishop wafted him away to be Priest in Charge of St. Saviour's, Georgetown, and then Rector of Leguan and Essequibo Islands. Later still, in 1968, the parish of Bartica Missions was broken up, and a large portion became the parish of Kamarang under John Dorman, while Richard Cole returned to Bartica as Vicar. Fr Eric Pocklington, CMP, whom the Archbishop had met in Africa, came to Guyana in 1961 to be Vicar of St. Philip's, Georgetown. He had one curate already, but he was allowed to have another, a CMP member, Fr Paul Adamson. This priest was later priest of the wide-stretching Rupununi parish. Here he found himself the administrator of a cattle ranch, and in spite of the fact that that is not a subject usually dealt with in theological colleges, he acquitted himself very well as did one or two successors. In case some El Dorado reader, unused to the weird and wonderful ways of Guyana, should enquire why it was needful for these priests to take up this work, the answer is that the colonial regime had ruled that no outsider should take up residence in the Savannah unless he was the owner or lessee of a cattle ranch.

After Richard Cole left Bartica and had three years in England he came back to Guyana in 1975, and was appointed to St. Matthew's, East Bank, Demerara and to St. Anne's. When he was to go on long leave, he obtained the help of Donald Percy CMP to look after these parishes in his absence. In doing this, Donald won golden opinions. This taste of Guyana, which he had then, was to bear fruit in the future. Then the need to have the tribes of the Interior looked after by priests from their own tribes became evident, and the Alan Knight Training Centre was set up at Yupukari, Rupununi. CMP was appealed to for priests to come and take charge. Brian Doolan CMP, volunteered, and later the above Donald Percy came forward to join him. They ran the first three-year course at the Centre with Donald also looking after the huge Rupununi parish. Their efforts were crowned with success when 12 men were ordained to the priesthood in 1986. After an interval, when CMP had again been asked to provide two priests, the second course started. John Twisleton the centre had a Principal that many an English educational institution might have envied, he being an ex Fellow of St. John's, Oxford and a D.Phil. The other was Fr Allan Buik, a Scot, proud of that fact. The difficulties of running the course at Yupukari had in the meantime increased; nevertheless, six men were ready to be ordained priest in 1990. Fr Twisleton left CMP in the course of the training period, but Fr Buik, still CMP, has returned to Guyana for further duties mainly concerned with the training of honorary priests. Two Wardens of CMP have visited Guyana. The late Fr Pears CR, came in 1962 and stayed at Bartica. He was an authority on insect-life, and he much enjoyed himself, darting about with his butterfly net on a small island like a seven-year-old. The other was the late Fr. George Sidebottom CR who dutifully came to visit the CMP priest at Bartica but got involved with the pressing crowds of the Holy Saturday steamer going up the Essequibo. Fr Derek Lowe's very active ministry in Guyana at All Saints', New Amsterdam, and in the Berbice River Missions, especially his remodelling and furnishing of St. Peter in Chains Church, and Sandhills, should be noted. At that time he was not a member of CMP, but has been one for some long time now'.

Fr Richard Cole (30)

Fr Leslie Rooney 1917-1993

Leslie Francis Rooney, priest, born 1917, died in his sleep on the night of November 6th 1993. After ordination at Durham in 1940 and a curacy at Harton, he went to Guyana and served a second curacy at St. Philip's Georgetown before becoming Vicar of the vast parish of Bartica, Essequibo, with many missions up the great rivers Mazaruni, Cuyuni and their tributaries eventually to be the first to open the - missions at Kamarang. Here the work he began, is being carried on by Canon John Dorman and Amerindian priests trained at the Alan Knight Centre. On his return to England he became Metropolitan area secretary for S.P.G., before becoming vicar of Benfleet (54-61). In 1961 until 1964 he was chaplain and tutor of St. Mark's College, Mapanza. From 1964-66 he was chaplain of St. Mary Magdalene School, Richmond, Chaplain to the Hostel of God, Southwark 1966-71. Until he retired he was teaching at the Cathedral School, Exeter and was Public Preacher in the Diocese of Exeter. During a long retirement he was active in support of his first love, Guyana and tireless in supporting the work there. Sadly, a year ago his dear wife Rita died in her sleep and Leslie retreated to a retirement home where he quickly made, in a short time, his mark and where he was very happy. He was a B.Sc. of London University, B.D.and A.K.C. When at Bartica, he prepared a small book of prayers for the parish and called it 'Come, Come and Adore'. This has passed through many editions and for years has been a standby in all parts of the Diocese. It is likely to be his abiding memorial, there, where so many hearts will be warmed and saddened, when the news of his going from us is received. Our sympathy goes out to his surviving brother. May Leslie and Rita rest in peace.' (31)

The Footsteps of Mission in Guyana Fr John Tearnan

'For the past three years since 1997 Guyana has been home for me. I served and ministered as priest in the church of St Saviour, Charlestown, an in-the-ghetto parish not far from La Penitence Market, and the Demerara River. The church, even now, is known as the Chinese Church, yet many Chinese have left both the parish and the country. James, a 28 year-old African-Guyanese, was confirmed the day I arrived in the parish. He lived, like many others from the Lot right next to the church, in a one-roomed home with his wife, his three children, and his father. Most Sundays, he was in church when his work as a stevedore let him. His daughters came with him, and his youngest, James, was baptised in the church. He had asked to be given the Word of God, and to be taught the things of the Almighty. Christ was changing his life in the midst of an environment of poverty, alcohol, drugs, and crime. But now, three years later, his body lies in a grave. James died from injuries when he was struck down by a swinging container on the wharf where he worked. His wife, Denise, was baptised on my last Sunday in the parish as its priest. Such a tale tells of the footsteps through the joy and agony of Christian mission, steps that are always touched with eternity.

Jesus says 'I was in prison and you came to me'. Such words have taken me to prison, and to men on Death Row. In that exacting situation, mission is to share the word and the love of God, his forgiveness and redemption. It meant being with men as they prepare to die and being with them at the moment of execution. There in the midst of prison it is both to preach and to be the word or, rather, to be and then to preach the Word, and to be ready to be bread broken for others. There are tales of mission to tell- of the dawning of the light of faith in Christ, of the healing of deep inner hurts, of reconciling relationships, of peace and love and joy in human lives, in the lives of others and my own.

Returning to Guyana in October, 1997, I am to become, by the Bishop's appointing, travelling Superintendent of Interior Missions. That means to go and be with the Amerindian people of God, in their villages, parishes, and churches, and with their priests. Most live in the hinterland, the interior of Guyana, along the western frontier of the country, people with their own culture and languages, their village and social organisation, their own farming and economic system. The Gospel has been preached, and mission churches, Christian communities established, yet, as always, there is the nurturing of faith and life of priest and missionaries, to link up with the priests, who since being ordained, have worked often on their own, because where they are ministering and serving, there is little means of communication. The priests may only see each other once or twice a year. when Synod is held in Georgetown. As I prepare for this new mission, it looks very much as if I am to travel by plane, by boat, horse, ox cart, on foot, by bike, or by 4 x 4. Such travel is going to need financial resources if the mission is ever to become a reality. There is much excitement among the priests at this new mission especially as communities in which they work feel very much under threat. One hundred years ago, gold and diamonds were discovered in the interior and the 'rush' has been on ever since, bringing a constant stream of newcomers to the interior. For the Amerindians this has been mostly disastrous. The newcomers want the men for their skills and labour, and the women for their kitchens and hammocks. Big money is earned and close on its heels comes alcohol, drugs, sex and disease, all elements of destruction. So the challenge is enormous, not only to preach the Word of God, but to live it, and to extend its work and power for peace and love, to heal, to redeem, to make whole, to reconcile. So this new mission is being with the people, in their villages, in their homes, in their churches, to share the word of God with them, to break the bread, and to know Christ in both. It is to listen, to understand, to learn of their hopes and fears, their joys and sorrows, their faith and doubts, their needs, and to stay with their hurts, with the pain as it really is, where it really is, and together to discover what Christ is willing for all his people. As more and more is heard and understood, so more clearly the needs and the resources to meet those needs will be discerned - teaching and training materials, practical resources - solar lights, radios, audio video equipment, people. So let ears hear, minds seek, hearts love and pray, and hands give. This mission is more than my mission. It is our mission, but, above all, it is Christ's mission, in which we all have a part to play, and we have his footsteps in which to place our own.' (32)

9   The Twisleton Venture

Anne Twisleton writes: 'Father Allan Buik and Father John Twisleton were two of the students in USPG's College of the Ascension, where I had gone to do two terms of mission study in 1986. There were several colleges in Selly Oak, Birmingham each with a different character, Quaker, Baptist, High Church Anglican, Evangelical, Methodist. All of the students gathered for lectures on various aspects of overseas service. The lecturers and their theology were very diverse, and so were the backgrounds of the students, bursary students from Africa, India, and other parts of the world as well as Brits, other Europeans and Americans. I was at Selly Oak with my two sons, David (11) and John (9), having been appointed to be on the staff of the Anglican Bishop of Argentina as Diocesan Secretary in Buenos Aires. The boys went to local schools and we all lived in a flat at the College. I had been a widow for 7 years, after my first husband Robert died in Ecuador, where we worked for a Christian Radio Station broadcasting programmes in 15 or more languages to North and South America, Europe, Japan, Russia and its satellite nations. John Twisleton had been appointed as the Principal of the Allan Knight Training Centre, in Guyana, South America, and Allan was going to help him train up 12 Amerindian men to be Anglican priests, to serve their own communities. As my boys inquisitively wandered round the college on the day we arrived at the college and I was unpacking the luggage, they met John Twisleton, and introduced me to him. We became friends, and all of us went to the cinema, or on walks. We kept the relationship low key.

Allan and John were making lists of books and equipment to set up the training centre, they would be running. I helped type the inventory, which included Mass sets, rosaries, incense, theological tomes, crucifixes and statues of saints, clerical robes and chasubles and scarves, boxes of communion wafers. In all, they shipped 63 wooden crates to Guyana, which had then to be flown by small plane to the

74

Rupununi Savannahs, to the village of Yupukari where there was a school, a church and a barn like vicarage, as well as the adobe huts with thatched roofs of the villagers. A land rover was also purchased, as the nearest town, Lethem, was a 2 hour drive away in the dry season, and 5 hours when the rains set in. After he left Selly Oak in 1987 John's letters were soon coming through when he arrived in Guyana, first to me and the boys in the UK, and then, when we arrived in Buenos Aires, to our address in Argentina. The life John and Allan were living was one devoid of luxuries, and often of basic food. Letters would arrive saying, "There's been a measles outbreak - 50 children in the area have died" "the men didn't kill anything last night, so it was bare rice again". The wives of the students were from several different languages and tribes, and there was tension between them and the locals at times, and great homesickness. There were many deaths, of babies born sickly, of fever, measles, appendicitis, accidents, but rarely of old age. As I read the letters, I was profoundly thankful to be living in the suburbs of Buenos Aires, and commuting into the city to work in the Diocesan Office at the Anglican Cathedral. My boys were given scholarships to a good school thanks to the Bishop, and were soon chattering in Spanish (half remembered from our years in Ecuador) and catching buses, playing football with the neighbours and enjoying the friendly church we became part of.

Because the conditions in the interior were pretty basic, USPG gave John and Allan a good break after the first few months, paying for an air ticket to wherever they could best recuperate. Allan opted to go to Barbados, and John asked if he could fly to Argentina and stay with us for a couple of weeks. During John's stay in Buenos Aires he met all the clergy and staff I was working with, and the Bishop and his wife. They liked John, and asked why when we were obviously in love, we were not thinking about marriage? Having read so many accounts of the difficulties of living in Yupukari, I was even more thankful to be living in BA, but the Bishop's wife, who had married Bishop Richard in the middle of Africa, overruled, and sent John back to Guyana to ensure that there would be provision for me - ie, a toilet at least! The Missionary Society I was being paid by, USPG, agreed we could marry, after both Alan Buik and Bishop Randolph George agreed, the latter observing the benefits of having a married priest on the AKTC team given the need for support and teaching for the wives of the students. I travelled from Buenos Aires with the boys - by coach, train, plane and finally land rover, and our parents travelled from Yorkshire to attend our wedding, landing in Georgetown, and from there by small plane over the rain forest and into the savannahs. After our wedding in St Mary's Church at Yupukari, the village put on a party in the school house, with my parents and John's mother. The women had been preparing Cari (a home-made cassava brew for days - it was pretty strong!). The party went on long into the night, but Allan was to drive us to our honeymoon hotel, so we climbed into the land rover and set off on the hour or so's journey. That's when the long awaited rainy season began, with a vengeance, and the hard dry savannahs (no paved roads) turned to deep mud. The LR got bogged down, and in my wedding dress, white stockings and high heels, I had to climb down and help to push the vehicle out of the mud. We finally managed to winch it out, but couldn't undo the rope, so had to leave it for our parents to retrieve next day. The spot has been nicknamed 'Honeymoon swamp'. The idea was that Allan would take us to Pirara and return to Yupukari, but instead the torrential rain meant that he had to stay in the ranch overnight, and join us for breakfast next morning! Later on our parents and the boys also turned up and stayed for a coffee. Allan had every right to feel put out when instead of working in partnership with John, he found himself in a house of his own, albeit yards from the vicarage. He took it in good part, and he had that invaluable instinct of a bachelor to turn up just as I took biscuits or scones out of the oven, and we had many an evening drinking rum with Allan, and many a crowded journey in the land rover with up to a dozen locals plus babies. The babies were flung into the air when a particularly large hole in the road bounced the LR, and all the mothers scrambled to catch their own infants as they landed! A big crowd of villagers would try to squeeze into the vehicle whenever we made the trip to buy food in Lethem. When Allan had his 50th birthday, we opened a precious tin of ham, and some other goodies squirrelled away for a special occasion. We were eating the meal when we heard a lot of shouting. The villagers were drinking and someone came to the door to tell us there'd been a fight. A woman, rather drunk, had shoved her husband's hammock while he was lying in it. "Do that again and I'll cut you!" He said. She did it again, and he lifted his machete and slammed it down on her hand. Blood all over, and though the cuts across her fingers were bad, they hadn't severed her fingers. One of the other men had tackled the husband and held him firmly. The land rover was used to take the woman to the hospital in Lethem (which had no doctors, nurses or medicines, just a few metal beds with thin blankets on them). The husband was taken to jail. But not for long - it was said he'd bribed the police by telling them he would steal a cow from a neighbouring ranch. So the husband was home sooner than the wife, whose wounds took a long time to heal. Incredibly, the man said, "It was her fault - she shouldn't have pushed my hammock!" And the village women agreed with him!

All our water was brought from the river a mile away, and as gas was expensive, we did not boil it, but drank it, amoebas and all. The whole village went down to the river to bathe each evening, and to wash their clothes on convenient rocks, trying to avoid the sting rays, alligators, piranhas and other creatures in the black water, such as anacondas and giant otters. Bats roosted in the rafters of the vicarage and Allan's house - only the mosquito nets shielded us (more or less) from their droppings. Snakes were common. They were all assumed to be poisonous and the locals would dispatch them with their machetes. Sometimes a jaguar's footprints would be spotted, and on one occasion a dog, sleeping on a doorstep, was taken in the night. Allan was shaving one morning when a small snake popped its head through the overflow. On another occasion, as the students came for the very early service at the church, they all dipped their fingers in the holy water and crossed themselves. When it got lighter, a small snake was seen to be swimming happily in the stoop. Every day or two we inspected our feet and used a needle to dig out jiggers, which if not noticed would lay their eggs under our skin. The Amerindians travelled mainly on the river in dug out canoes to tend their farms, and to spear fish as they went. Bows and arrows were used to catch monkeys, wild pigs, and other creatures at night. An iguana might be the catch of the day, chopped up, intestines and all, and served up in a stew. And yes, it was as revolting as it sounds! Allan had his kilt, and on special occasions would dress up and dance on the school stage, much to the amusement of the villagers, who would catcall and shout -"Farder Allan mus' be a woman - he wearing a skirt!". My parents took David back to England to live with them after the wedding - he was approaching GCSEs and so needed to be in a British school. Young John, who has autism, stayed with us in Guyana, and thrived in the simple life where the local children were unsophisticated, and for the first time in his life John was a leader, climbing mango trees to pinch the fruit, playing football using a plastic bag filled with straw, jumping from branches into the river with the other boys, learning how to make a bow and arrow, learning to speak Macusi when he squatted around the cooking pot in the adobe huts where the families of the students dwelt. We also had a home schooling course provided by the Missionary Society, and John Sr and I took turns to apply the excellent programme, with books that the other boys enjoyed sharing. Letters to and from friends and relations at home were eagerly awaited - sometimes we'd go weeks without mail, if there was a shortage of petrol for the small planes to get to Lethem, or to a ranch 12 miles away.

John and I kept up our friendship with Allan after our return to the UK. A few years ago we were glad to be able to help him when he needed to move on from church property into the College of St Barnabas, Lingfield. Then, as he became unable to sustain himself there, he was moved into a care home. He seemed to be fairly peaceful, and joined in the familiar liturgy the 3 of us had together when we visited. He seemed resigned and quietly lived out his last days with dignity and peace. We will remember our colleague and friend with gratitude and love'. (33)

10   Venturesome faith

The village creek had turned white. Over a matter of weeks the Amerindian community of Tassarine off the Mazaruni River in Guyana had seen their water change colour. The source of pollution was undisputed. Not satisfied with their quest for gold in the main river, a hardy group of miners had pulled their dredge through the jungle upstream of the village to resume work. Nothing seems to be able to stop those crazed by the thought of finding gold, not even hundreds of Amerindians deprived of drinking water. Having invested three years of my life with USPG and the Diocese of Guyana training priests for the Amerindian communities I marked the 10th anniversary of their priestly ordinations in 1990 by returning to Guyana on two months' Sabbatical Leave from my post as Missioner in the London Diocese. My journey to Tassarine, Issano involved a six-hour journey on a 'jet-ski' sailing up the Mazaruni River from the coast. The craft built on two jet engine impellers had the extraordinary capacity to hop up the rapids and cut the journey to Issano from days to hours. As I was to discover, the new accessibility of the village to visitors was a mixed blessing. Around 1995 the villagers had been forced to move up a creek to Tassarine to avoid the pollution of their drinking water formerly taken from the Mazaruni River at Issano landing. Now in 2000 the miners had started to dredge upstream of the new village. The village captain and his assistant, a priest I helped train at AKTC, Fr. Allan Alfred, gave me a letter of protest to carry for them to the Ministry of Geology and Mines. It was received with concern at the Ministry, and a promise of attention. The government seeks to balance the encouragement of gold mining, with its return in hard currency, against the rights of the indigenous people. It is not easy for them to police developments from the coast so they welcomed the letter. Since his ordination Fr. Allan Alfred had been close to his people in their struggle for land rights. Like several of the Amerindian priests he works as a community leader, using his training to serve both the material and spiritual needs of his people. With his assistance the Anglican community in Tassarine was then in the vanguard of a struggle for a basic human right - drinking water. Whilst in Issano I won my missionary's 'Oscar' by getting bitten by a vampire bat. It was the season for a veritable plague of these blood-sucking creatures. Despite a night-light set up to ward off these creatures, I awoke around 1am with a burning sensation on my foot. There was a whirring noise and when I put on my torch a pool of blood on the bed. The bat had crawled under my net to take a chunk out of one of my toes. My encounter with the vampire, which bled me, became for me a parable of the struggle of my fellow Anglicans in the face of the rampant greed, which is bleeding them.

Anne and my venture of faith travelling as Anglican missionaries to Guyana to help train Amerindian priests was allied to a double edged venture by the ordinands themselves. They struggled venturing from home into a strange region at Yupukari. They struggled on their return to communities the poorer for 3 years without their leadership prey to the chances and chances of Guyana's interior with its communication problems. An English priest can have a car to help him. Fr. Allan at Issano had his father's "wood skin" and much paddling necessary to accomplish his ministry. What a privilege to sail along to the cries of toucans and the salute of giant blue butterflies flitting in and out of the surrounding forest or later, as I found, sailing with outboard along the Waini River catching glimpses or red orchids clinging to the trees and giant wild cocoa fruit hanging over the water. As the national anthem voices it, "Dear land of Guyana" indeed and the privilege to venture where few Guyanese ever manage to go was ours even if we had work to do. On my first visit to Kamarang to visit Canon John Dorman in 1987 I recall Fr Winston Williams paddling 11 hours in his woodskin just to meet me. The same year in Kaburi I recall first meeting Bishop - then Father - Alfred David. Out hunting just before I met him, Father had just fought off a leopard! An impressive, small but very powerful man, Alfred David then and now takes the quest for souls in his stride, a born hunter. I spent many hours travelling with him up the Potaro River, on one occasion clinging to a petrol tanker with a dozen people, tossed up and down a thousand times on the journey of a lifetime along the rough track to Tumatumari. There I was able to say Mass on the tenth anniversary of my priesting in Sheffield Cathedral July 1977. I felt I had literally come a long way from there. With the arrival of mobile phones and the Rupununi Road the communication problems have somewhat eased but they remain a challenge in many parts of Guyana especially with the ever rising cost of fuel.

On three Sabbatical visits in 1995, 2000, 2007 sponsored by USPG and GDA I engaged in situ with most of the clergy trained at the Alan Knight Training Centre bringing encouragement that built on the work of the Diocese and USPG missionaries like Fr John Tearnan. The interior clergy evidenced many examples of active social responsibility involving themselves over that period in Farmers' Cooperatives at Waramuri and Warapoka and a Community Resource Centre at Annai blessed by the Church. I recall Fr Mitchell Henry's struggles on his return from Yupukari to Kwebana in 1990 where his churches had seen the arrival of a logging company in his absence. His partnership with the local headmaster and village Captain established the right of the village council to collect royalties from the local saw mill. This enabled Kwebana's villagers to have a tractor, outboard and chainsaw as well as a radio in their Health Centre. Through the latter their Medex was able to conduct operations in an emergency with guidance from a coastal doctor. In his Synod Charges Bishop Randolph frequently paid special tribute to the ministry of the amerindian clergy and encouraged coastal parishes to forge links with interior churches. No one visiting Guyana's interior can be blind to the serious problems there like malaria, river pollution and uncontrolled logging and how the Anglican clergy trained through AKTC are in the vanguard of moves to address these issues. One sad fact of life in Guyana's interior are the Christian divisions. Areas once amicably divided into Anglican and Roman Catholic regions had by 2000 Baptist, Seventh Day Adventist, Full Gospel, Apostolic, Assemblies of God, Bible Missionary and Bahai Faith as well. Usually these groups have rich funding, sometimes from the U.S.A. In Waramuri an American lady I met had appeared with sewing machines announcing "I preach Christ not denominations." Alas her words have proved naive to put it in the kindest way. Of course sheep stray to where the grass is greenest. Those Anglican priests with a special preaching gift and a reputation for practising what they preached were least troubled by the sects. Many clergy however admitted then and now how challenged they feel especially by Christian groups funded heavily from overseas which often meant village families spreading their members across denominations to maximise material benefits.

In 2007 my impressions of both Georgetown and the Rupununi after 7 years was one of buoyancy. The World Cup cricket event that year had involved a general face lift for town. Traffic lights were working and most people were obeying them. In Annai the emergence of the Rupununi road meant more houses and schools and facilities including electricity in places. That year the Diocese had 35 priests, 15 working in the interior though one transferred to the coast. Fr. Charles Roland's ministry then proved a great encouragement with church attendance soaring in Bartica from around 40 to between 200 and 300 over a year or so. All the clergy I met felt too thinly spread on account of the overall shortage of priests. Coastal priests who had to hurry off to the next Sunday Mass were particularly frustrated by their inability to engage with the people after each celebration. I had to shop around to find weekday Masses. Among the encouragements reported at a coastal chapter meeting were the vibrancy of the Mother's Union and Brotherhood of St. Andrew who mobilise the laity in many parishes. Small groups were seen as a clue to revitalisation – prayer groups, bible study groups, Alpha groups, youth groups, MU, Brotherhood of St Andrew, Charismatic groups. Among mission and renewal strategies Lichfield had a PUSH plan: *Pray Until Something Happens*. From the

Essequibo Coast Fr. Rupert Osborne shared a strategy by which every member was asked to reach one lapsed member. At St. James, Kitty Fr. Evan Semple reported the regular contribution of a steel band within Sunday worship. Among constraints discussed among the clergy were frustration of youth caused by much Anglican reserve about having more lively worship. I was nevertheless able to have some discussions with Fr. Oscar Bazil, Bishop Randolph and youth leaders keen to develop youth led music groups. That year we held an interior clergy conference sponsored by GDA. It was primarily a listening exercise in which the 11 priests able to attend listened day by day to one another's joys and sorrows bringing some encouragement, repentance and healing. The stories from the priests included miracles, periods of depression, pressure on their families through their being priests, temptations to excess drinking, community cohesion broken by rival Christian groups and the increasing cost of transportation. Each morning I led a prayer school and in the afternoon an internet training session at Rock View, Annai. In the evening we followed through a Sacred Triduum as if from Maundy Thursday to Easter Sunday, an opportunity to refresh our conduct of Holy Week Liturgy whilst entering the Paschal mystery afresh ourselves. The clergy were able to look at best use of hymns in liturgy and to compile a hymn supplement that I made up on my return to the coast. The ministry to individuals seemed to remain a great strength of the interior churches compared to the coast. This was provided in Annai each night as up to a couple of hundred attended these evangelistic liturgies that ended with the provision of sacramental confession, healing prayer and prayer for renewal in the Holy Spirit. As a priest I have never heard as many confessions in such a short period. A similar evangelistic conference has continued over the years bringing priests and people together at different interior locations.

Anne and I visited Guyana 2011 at the invitation of Bishop Cornell Moss for me to conduct a two day pre-synod workshop for interior delegates and Anne a clergy wives' day retreat after Synod. The highpoint of our visit was attendance at Synod Mass in St Philip's where the Bishop issued a challenge based on Nehemiah 2.18 to rise up and rebuild the Church in the Diocese, to rebuild Guyana and, as a means to this, for members to rise from an external form of godliness into a new relationship with Our Lord. This solemn Mass involved catholic ritual, classical and Caribbean music, evangelical preaching and scores of young people in serving and ushering. It had been well prepared and the venue, so recently restored, was underlined as an example of church restoration to be emulated across the diocese. I returned to Guyana 2013 to be installed as a Canon in St George's Cathedral following my appointment as the Bishop's UK Commissary. The Bishop invited me to present arguments for and against the ordination of women before a vote required by Provincial Synod in 2015. Like his predecessor Bishop Moss was concerned that any move to ordain women should be seen as no innovation but as a development true to scripture, tradition and reason guided by the Holy Spirit and Christian consensus.

Conclusion

For everything there is a season, and a time for every matter under heaven Ecclesiastes 3:1 (NRSV)

Two centuries of Church of England mission to what is now Guyana have been 'a season' and the 90 years of GDA 'a time' now ending in closure. The latter links to a new season for the Guyana diaspora in which Christian enthusiasm first kindled abroad has failed to infect children and grandchildren brought up in the UK creating an ageing membership. This phenomenon has ended in the closing of a number of Diocesan Associations and not just GDA. The Anglocatholic stream of the Church of England, a key factor in kindling vocations like those of Alan Knight, John Dorman and Derek Goodrich, has also lost energy and membership through being put on the back foot by changes like the ordination of women. The loss of Christian allegiance among youth both in the UK Guyana diaspora and Guyana itself links to a difficult season for Christians worldwide whose divisions are more exposed. Adept with electronic media and less into physical religious gatherings young people are aware as never before of both religious diversity and hypocrisy. People see religions and other worldviews side by side and feel incapable of assessing their rival truth claims. The strong historical base of Christianity, unique among religions, in the well evidenced history, teaching, death and resurrection of Jesus falls foul of the crisis in truth telling and false news linked to electronic media's capacity to incessantly propagate untruth. This impacts assessing Christianity not least its sexual ethics that chafe with young people as much today as ever. The relentless social media exposure of the failures of bishops and priests in that realm is something of a tsunami sweeping away faith's credibility. More profoundly, the material benefits now available in both the UK and Guyana distract many from the primacy of the spiritual realm and the need for God. Nevertheless in hardship, as through the COVID pandemic and conflicts like that in Ukraine, we see people young and old waking up to faith. In the letter to the Hebrews 12:27-28 the writer interprets to readers going through hard times as being 'the removal of what is shaken - that is, created things - so that what cannot be shaken may remain... a kingdom that cannot be shaken' (NRSV). This is the best context in which to evaluate the ending of GDA which does not subtract from the ongoing growth of God's kingdom in both Guyana and the UK.

In my introduction I recalled my missionary call to a land famous for its fishing with rivers teaming with fish and people in good numbers readily caught up into worship when there is a priest 'to fish for people'. Even on my most recent visits to Guyana in 2015 and 2016 congregations I served on the coast were in hundreds compared to the dozens familiar in most of the English parishes I now serve as itinerant supply priest. As captured particularly in the Chapter on Dean-emeritus Derek Goodrich the greater scale of things in the Church in Guyana has been part of its drawing power to missionaries from England. On our return from Guyana Derek and I continued to play leading roles in GDA supporting the work of the Church in the Diocese of Guyana as invited by the Bishop. As GDA membership declined there were less personnel ready or suitably gifted to be invited. Canon Edwin and Marlene Edwards played a significant role alongside myself at the invitation of Bishop Moss. The latter challenged the Diocese to take more responsibility for its own finances through members giving a tithe of their income. Coincident with this challenge GDA gradually pulled back from paying the Diocese's Provincial Quota and expenses associated with the Bishop's car. The premature death in 2015 of Bishop Cornell Moss was followed by the appointment of Bishop Charles Davidson in 2016. The change of Bishop coincided with loss of GDA committee members, notably Jane Garner in 2017, the loss of whose generous service for 21 years as administrative secretary was deeply felt. GDA members flocked to Southwark Cathedral 26 February 2019 to see the Archbishop of Canterbury commission Guyanese

Sheran Harper as the first Mothers' Union Worldwide President appointed from overseas. After the Diocese of Guyana Synod voted to ordain women priests GDA Treasurer Canon Roxanne Hunte was invited by Bishop Davidson in 2020 to help post-ordination training of Mother Rita Hunter at Jawalla. The closing meeting of GDA on 24 June 2021 was buoyed up by the appointment of the first Amerindian Bishop and sent congratulations to the Revd Canon Alfred David on his forthcoming consecration as Suffragan Bishop of Kamarang on August 24, 2021 in St George's Cathedral by the Archbishop of the West Indies with other bishops. Bishop Davidson held a thanksgiving for GDA on 25 August, appropriately the day after Bishop-elect David's consecration.

Christian mission is an overflow of faith and this book captures something of that overflow from the Church of England to Guyana of which I am privileged to be part of. Figures like William Austin, Alan Knight, John Dorman and Derek Goodrich capture that dynamic linked to the highpoint of the mid twentieth century anglocatholic movement within the Church of England. The rise and fall of the Guyana Diocesan Association is linked both to the decline of that movement and to the establishing of the Diocese of Guyana as more fully indigenous. 'Guyana Venture' tells part of one side of a story. It is partial because it is based on my limited perspective. Though a Canon of the Diocese of Guyana I have no oversight of the Diocese that honoured me and have spent most of my ministry in the UK. It is one-sided because it is an avowedly Church of England perspective making the best of the chequered history of colonialism which impacts UK-Guyanese relations to this day. The book aims to complement my friend Blanche Duke's History of the Anglican Church in Guyana. I seized the opportunity to frame the history of the Church of England mission to Guyana because that mission has framed my life through encountering John Dorman and its consequences including marriage to Anne at Yupukari in 1988. Her vivid description of our time there captures the beauty and challenge of Guyana's interior as do the passages detailing the courage and struggles of the saintly John Dorman. Guyana has been to me both venture and adventure, both set within the overflow of venturesome faith seeking to make the meaning and power of the word of God and the eucharist available to all, in season and out of season.

Notes

1   Blanche Emmeline Duke, A History of the Anglican Church in Guyana (Know Your Diocese), Red Thread Women's Press (Georgetown), 2000

2   Savannah Special, A magazine put together by the staff and students of the Alan Knight Training Centre, Yupukari, Rupununi Easter 1990 p5

3   Blanche Duke, A History of the Anglican Church in Guyana p65, p69-70, p318

4   Blanche Duke, A History of the Anglican Church p17, p41

Ms 5   Blanche Duke, A History of the Anglican Church p46-47

5   Derek Goodrich, The Words and Works of Alan John Knight (Derek Goodrich, 1999) p173

7

https://en.wikipedia.org/wiki/St._George%27s_Cathedral,_Georgetown

8   Derek Goodrich, The Words and Works of Alan John Knight p198

9   Derek Goodrich, The Words and Works of Alan John Knight p16-17

10   Derek Goodrich, The Words and Works of Alan John Knight p3

11   Derek Goodrich, The Words and Works of Alan John Knight p49-50, p135, p144, p148, p183-184

12   El Dorado, The Magazine of the Guyana Diocesan Association, September 1968

13   https://www.britannica.com/place/Guyana/History

14   Derek Goodrich, The Words and Works of Alan John Knight p138

15   Blanche Duke, A History of the Anglican Church in Guyana p416-7

16   Everard F IM Thurn, Among the Indians of Guiana (London, 1883) p140

17   http://www.missionpriests.com/a-bit-of-history.html

18   Derek Goodrich, Old-Style Missionary - The Ministry of John Dorman, Priest in Guyana (Tavener Publications, 2003)

19   Church Times Obituary: The Very Revd Derek Goodrich 19 November 2021

20   Derek Goodrich, The Ramblings of a Parish Priest (Derek Goodrich, 1995) p15

21   Derek Goodrich, More Ramblings of a Parish Priest (Dynamic Graphics, 2011)
p26

22   Blanche Duke, A History of the Anglican Church in Guyana p80-81

23   Derek Goodrich, More Ramblings of a Parish Priest p21, p67, p83

24   Church Times Obituary: The Very Revd Derek Goodrich 19 November 2021

25   http://johntwisleton.blogspot.com/2021/09/fr-derek-goodrich-funeral-homily-canon.html

26   USPG Project News, Diocese of Guyana, Yupukari: The Alan Knight Training Centre, Project Number 266, Bulletin Number 3 June 1983

27   El Dorado, April 1998 p12-13

28   El Dorado, November 2009 p18

29   El Dorado, May 1996 p11-12

30   El Dorado, November 1990 p13-14

31   El Dorado, November 1993 p16

32   El Dorado, November 1997 p16-17

33   Anne Twisleton Letter to Fr Allan Buik's nephew 10 April 2020

About the Author

John Twisleton is an ideas and people person, theologian and pastor, ministering in Sussex. He broadcasts on London-based Premier Christian Radio and is well known as an author and blogger. Canon Twisleton has served as Principal of the Alan Knight Training Centre for indigenous clergy in Guyana's interior, Commissary for the Bishop of Guyana and Secretary of Guyana Diocesan Association.

Books by the Author

A History of St Giles Church, Horsted Keynes

Besides being the burial place of former UK Prime Minister Harold Macmillan (1894-1986) and mystic ecumenist Archbishop Robert Leighton (1611-1684) St Giles, Horsted Keynes has association with the history of Sussex back to the 8th century. As 53rd Rector (2009-2017) John Twisleton wrote this illustrated history with the assistance of church members.

Baptism - Some Questions Answered

Illustrated booklet on infant baptism used across the Anglican Communion. It explains the commitments involved in baptising a baby, challenges hypocrisy and attempts to clear up a number of misunderstandings in popular culture about what baptism is all about.

Christianity - Some Questions Answered

This booklet for Christian enquirers attempts dialogue between Christianity and its contemporary critics. A brief inspection of Christian faith clarifies both its unique claims and its universal wisdom so they can be seen and owned more fully.

Confession - Some Questions Answered

Illustrated booklet explaining the value of sacramental confession as an aid to spiritual growth. It commends confession as a helpful discipline serving people as they struggle against sin and guilt and seek to renew church membership.

Elucidations - Light on Christian controversies

As an Anglocatholic priest who experienced a faith crisis enlarging God for him, John Twisleton, former scientist, sheds light on thoughtful allegiance to Christianity in the 21st century condensing down thinking on controversial topics ranging from self-love to unanswered prayer, Mary to antisemitism, suffering to same sex unions, charismatic experience to the ordination of women, hell to ecology and trusting the Church, a total of twenty five essays.

Empowering Priesthood

This book is an enthusiastic presentation about the gift and calling of the ministerial priesthood. It argues that the choosing and sending of priests is vital to the momentum of mission and that their representation of Christ as priest, prophet and shepherd is given to help build love, consecrate in truth and bring empowerment to the whole priestly body of Christ.

Entering the Prayer of Jesus

Audio CD and booklet prepared by John Twisleton with the Diocese of Chichester and Premier Christian Radio providing spiritual wisdom from across the whole church. Contains audio contributions from Pete Greig (24-7 Prayer), Jane Holloway (Evangelical Alliance), Christopher Jamison (Worth Abbey), Molly Osborne (Lydia Fellowship) and Rowan Williams (Archbishop of Canterbury).

Experiencing Christ's Love

A wake up call to the basic disciplines of worship, prayer, study, service and reflection helpful to loving God, neighbour and self. Against the backdrop of the message of God's love John Twisleton presents a rule of life suited to enter more fully the possibilities of God.

Fifty Walks from Haywards Heath

Sub-titled 'A handbook for seeking space in Mid Sussex' this book celebrates the riches of a town at the heart of Sussex. Through detailed walk routes with schematic illustrations John Twisleton outlines routes from one to thirteen miles with an eye to local history and replenishment of the spirit.

Firmly I Believe

Forty talks suited to Christians or non-Christians explaining the creed, sacraments, commandment and prayer engaging with misunderstandings and objections to faith and its practical expression. Double CD containing 40 easily digested 3 minute talks accompanied by reflective music with full text in the accompanying booklet.

Forty Walks from Ally Pally

John Twisleton explores the byways of Barnet, Camden, Enfield and Haringey with an eye to green spaces, local history and a replenishment of the spirit. The routes, which vary in length between one mile and twenty miles, exploit the public transport network, and are well designed for family outings. The author provides here a practical handbook for seeking space in North London.

Healing - Some Questions Answered

An examination of the healing ministry with suggested ecumenical forms for healing services. The booklet addresses divine intervention, credulity, lay involvement, evil spirits and the healing significance of the eucharist.

Holbrooks History

Illustrated booklet compiled by John Twisleton with members of St Luke's Church, Holbrooks in Coventry about their parish and its church. It describes a multicultural community that has welcomed Irish, West Indian, Eastern European and Indian workers over the last century. The book includes dramatic pictures from the Second World War when the community and its church suffered bomb damage.

Meet Jesus

In a world of competing philosophies, where does Jesus fit in? How far can we trust the Bible and the Church? What difference does Jesus make to our lives and our communities? Is Jesus really the be all and end all? John Twisleton provides a lively and straightforward exploration of these and other questions pointing to how engaging with Jesus expands both mind and heart.

Moorends and its Church

Illustrated booklet telling the tale of the Doncaster suburb of Moorends from the sinking of the pit in 1904 to the 1984-5 mining dispute under the theme of death and resurrection. It includes a community survey of the needs of the elderly, young people and recreational and spiritual needs.

Pointers to Heaven

Completed at the height of COVID 19 this book condenses philosophical, theological and life insight into ten pointers to heaven troublesome to materialists: goodness, truth and beauty pointing to perfection alongside love, suffering, holy people and visions pointing beyond this world. If heaven makes sense of earth it is presented as doing so through such pointers, complemented by scripture, the resurrection and the eucharist, preview of the life to come.

Thirty Walks from Brighton Station

Distilling wisdom from the author's long association with Brighton & Hove this is a practical handbook for exploring the city and its surroundings reaching beyond the daytripper's duo of Pier and Pavilion to two hundred and sixty three sights. Subtitled 'Catching sights and sea air' the walks are listed in order of length from one mile up to fifteen. Detailed walk routes are provided alongside schematic illustrations to give the feel of each walk and its sights.

Using the Jesus Prayer

The Jesus Prayer of Eastern Orthodoxy, 'Lord Jesus Christ, Son of God, have mercy on me a sinner' offers a simple yet profound way of deepening spiritual life. John Twisleton gives practical guidance on how to use it outlining the simplification of life it offers.

More at Twisleton.co.uk

Printed in Great Britain
by Amazon

22533465R00057